First published in 2015 by
The British Library
96 Euston Road
London NW1 2DB

Cataloguing in publication data
atalogue record for this book is available
from the British Library

ISBN 978 0 7123 5782 1

Designed and typeset by
Briony Hartley, Goldust Design
Printed in Malta by
Gutenberg Press

INTRODUCTION

How to Skin a Lion is a collection of lost and outmoded advice that invites the reader to marvel at the treasury of useful information contained in the vast archives of the British Library. Medieval manuscripts, Victorian manuals and self-help guides of the early twentieth century have been mined to offer up the choicest nuggets of advice.

How to Skin a Lion aims to reveal the secrets of lost arts (such as how to train a falcon, or how to ride side-saddle); remind us how far modern conveniences have changed our lives (how to dry clean clothes, how to survive without a fridge); recall the complexities of etiquette (how to afford introductions, how to address a maharajah); highlight changing attitudes and beliefs (how to read the future with snails, how to fashion an elephant's foot into something useful); and furnish us with still-useful tips and guidance (how to treat a snake bite, how to cure seasickness).

Readers, however, should be advised that some pieces of advice contained herein have stood the test of time better than others, but part of the joy is to reflect on how much has changed (or in some cases, how little). Some of the items may inspire awe, others disdain; some may amuse or defy belief, but each extract will spark admiration for those who have gone before us.

To maintain the spirit of the sourcebooks, extracts retain the original spelling and punctuation, which at times is somewhat archaic. However, it preserves the voice of the original author, conjuring up some truly wonderful mental images of what these wise counsellors might have been like.

And so I open up this treasure box of outmoded advice for the reader to explore, enabling their mind to expand, boggle and delight in equal measure.

LIST OF ILLUSTRATIONS

All illustrations from the British Library unless otherwise stated.

How to cure sea-sickness

The blight of many a first-time sailor, sea-sickness, has been a problem throughout the ages. Edmund CP Hull shared this rather jolly sounding treatment in his 1874 book *The European in India*:

In case of probably sea-sickness – that most depressing of all disorders – or other indisposition, several little comforts, not always easily procurable on board ship, should be kept at hand. I recommend the following supply: – A pound or two of really good strong-flavoured tea; one or two tins of biscuits and gingerbread nuts; also of chocolate; and one or two favourite jams or marmalade. For sea-sickness there is no general specific, though some remedies are occasionally found very efficacious. Champagne, Moselle, or sparkling hock, are often found to have an excellent effect in settling the stomach; and a small case of pint or half-pint bottles of either, would probably therefore be of valuable acquisition. A bottle or two of really good port or sherry would not be amiss in cases of subsequent prostration.

For cases where copious amounts of alcohol has not done the trick, Hull offered the following rather less jolly option.

For persons much upset, and who find it impossible to take ordinary food or even delicacies, the following hints will prove invaluable. Take a fresh egg (of which every good passenger vessel will have an ample supply) and break it into a wine glass; add a few drops of vinegar, and a little black pepper from the cruet, and gulp down as in eating an oyster. This will be found wonderfully sustaining.

How to escape from fire

Household Management by 'An Old Housekeeper' (1877) contains this timeless advice on how to escape from a house-fire.

1. Be careful to acquaint yourself with the best means of exit from the house, both at the top and bottom.
2. On the first alarm, reflect before you act; if in bed at the time wrap yourself in a blanket or bedside carpet; open no more doors or windows than are absolutely necessary, and shut every door after you.
3. There is always from eight to twelve inches of pure air close to the ground; so if you cannot walk upright through the smoke, drop on your hands and knees, and thus go on. A wetted silk handkerchief, a piece of flannel, or a worsted stocking drawn over the face permits breathing and, to a great extent, excludes smoke.
4. If you can neither make your way upwards or downwards, get into a front room; if there is a family, see that they are all collected here. And keep the door closed as much as possible, as the smoke always follows the draught.
5. On no account throw yourself, or allow others to throw themselves from the windows. If no assistance is at hand,

and you are in extremity, tie the sheets together, and having fastened one end to some heavy piece of furniture, let down the women and children, one by one, by tying the end of the line of sheets round the waist, and lowering them through the window over the door, rather than over the area. You can then let yourself down, when the helpless are saved.

6. If a woman's clothes should catch fire, let her roll herself over on the ground; if a man be present, let him throw her down, if necessary, and wrap her in a rug, coat or anything at hand.

7. Bystanders, the instant they see a fire, should run for the fire-escape (or to the police station, if that should be nearer) where a jumping-sheet is always ready.

8. On the first discovery of a fire, it is of the utmost consequence to shut and keep shut, all the doors, windows, or other openings.

How to communicate with flowers

In the days when openly talking with a member of the opposite sex was frowned upon, people were forced to find other ways in which to liaise. *The Etiquette of Flowers* (1852) allows us a glimpse of how young lovers might have communicated with one another by sending posies of flowers, each with their own special meaning.

It is unclear who came up with this complicated code, but the book includes a series of elaborate rules that surely must have led to much confusion and misunderstanding.

If the flower, or plant, is intended to be preceded by the pronoun I, it must be presented in a position inclined towards the left hand. If it is to express thee or you it should incline to the right. As for example, a convolvulus and dahlia presented with an inclination to the left, convey the sentiment, I am bound by honor, or honor binds me, but to the right, thou art bound by honor.

The affirmative and negative are expressed according to the above Rule. For instance Lavender and Ivy presented inclining to the right would say 'I distrust your friendship' – but inclining to the left, I distrust not your friendship.

The sentiments, virtues, or vices represented by flowers in this vocabulary, are generally understood to be nouns, but it is as easy to change them into verbs, adjectives, or adverbs, as to affix the pronouns. If you desire the flower to be understood as a verb, put a red silken thread round the stem, just under the blossom, – if an adjective or a participle, a blue thread, and a yellow thread, if to be used as an adverb.

Flowers placed on the head signify anxiety regarding the subject of which it may be the emblem – on the lips secrecy, on the heart love, on the breast weariness.

The rules conveyed, the lover may now select a bloom to represent their secret feelings, presumably in the hope that the intended recipient of their posy also owns the same book and thus may be able to decipher the intention. Some of the flower meanings contained in *The Etiquette of Flowers* (1852) are as follows.

Aloe – *affliction, grief*
Basil, sweet – *hatred*
Bluebell – *constancy*
Buttercup – *ingratitude*
Cactus – *warmth*
Camomile – *energy in adversity*
Carnation – *women's love*
Carnation, striped – *refusal*
Carnation, yellow – *disdain*
Citron – *beauty with ill humour*
Daffodil – *regard*
Daisy – *cheerfulness*
Dogwood blossom – *I am perfectly indifferent to you*
Elder – *compassion*
Gooseberry – *anticipation*
Hellebore – *female inconstancy*
Iris, yellow – *flame, passion*
Lettuce – *cold hearted*
Mistletoe – *obstacles*
Pineapple – *keep your promises*
Poppy, white – *sleep*
Rose, dog – *pleasure and pain*
Rose, red – *beauty*
Rosemary – *remembrance*
Tulip, variegated – *beautiful eyes*
Turnip – *charity*
Wolfsbane – *misanthropy*

The manual goes on to describe some flowers that can communicate whole sentences.

I esteem but do not love you – spiderwort
I engage you for the next dance – ivy geranium
I am dazzled by your charms – ranunculus
I am poor but happy – vernal grass
My best days are past – meadow saffron
You are always lovely – double Indian pink
Am I forgotten? – holly

With this knowledge, giving flowers may never have the same happy simplicity again (especially as one may be desperately leafing through the book trying to work out what a bunch of sweet basil, yellow carnations and dogwood blossom tied with a green ribbon means).

How to dye silk, woollens &c. with indigo (French method)

In the days before synthetic dyes a true blue dye was a sought-after commodity. The Europeans had previously relied on woad to create blue tones, but in the fifteenth century, when a sea route to India opened up, the superior quality of Indian indigo superseded any local dyes. The *Indigofera tinctoria* plant is native to India, and the indigo dye is extracted by fermenting the leaves of the plant. The demand for indigo grew across Europe, so much so that indigo became known as 'blue gold' and the cultivation of the plant spread from India to the New World. It was only in 1897 that a synthetic and easily produced blue dye was created that effectively ended the indigo trade. *The Family Dyer and Scourer* by William Tucker (1817) offers the following recipe to dye items a charming blue hue.

Take four pounds of East India indigo, well pounded and sifted, put them into one gallon of vinegar, which must be set over a slow fire, twenty-four hours, to dissolve. At the expiration of this time, if the indigo is not sufficiently dissolved, pound it in a mortar with the liquor, adding now and then a little urine; afterwards put into it half a pound of the best madder. Mix these well, and pour them into a deal cask, containing sixty gallons of urine; mix well again, and stir them well morning and evening for eight days, till the liquor is green, and when stirred produces froth. It may then be worked immediately, always stirring it beforehand. This vat remains good till the dying wares are entirely exhausted, and will dye silks blue by dipping them in warm water, and then putting them in the vat for a longer or shorter time as the colour may be required. Deep purples and mazarine blues must first be passed through archil [a purple dye obtained from lichen] *and hot water: then in the vat, and then in the archil, and so proceed till you have obtained the desired colour.*

Obtaining the required sixty gallons of urine may well put off the modern dye enthusiast from trying this method.

How to stalk a lion

First, much like chasing out a pheasant, one must assemble a crowd of beaters. Abel Chapman in his 1908 tome *On Safari* recounted the following.

We had with us a fair-sized crowd of natives – between forty and fifty human beings, Swahili porters, askaris armed with Sniders, hunters, tent-boys, and the usual components of what is called a 'safari' or caravan. These we thought would make a useful troop of beaters; but they hardly viewed the undertaking with the same enthusiasm. A Swahili has his good points, but he is not a born sportsman, nor is he any longer a true savage. He wears clothes of sorts, drinks when he has a chance and can reckon up how many rupees go to a sovereign. The true savage, such as the Masai, does none of these things. Any reluctance to act as beaters was, however, soon dispelled by the forceful suasion of our 'headman,' Maguiar, the huge Soudanese, whose word, backed by the obvious power to enforce it, was law beyond debate; and after breakfast we set forth amidst deafening din.

Drums, tom-toms and rattles (fashioned from gourds filled with pebbles) were used to create a wall of sound, loud enough to startle even the most comatose of sleeping lions. The hunter must then crawl a fair distance behind the beaters in order to espy the lions disturbed by the noise. By beating from an area of cover to an area of clear ground the lions might be flushed out into the open, making a shot easier to take. But before the hunter can take aim, he must first ensure the conditions are favourable. Clive Phillipps-Wolley paints a vivid picture of how a traditional British big game hunter on safari might test the wind in his 1894 work *Big Game Shooting*.

It is … necessary to constantly test the wind. The most convenient and effectual way of doing this is to pick up and let fall from the hand a little sand, dust or pulverised leaves. On a very still calm day, when there is not enough wind to affect dust or dry leaves, a puff of smoke from a pipe or from a match, will serve the same purpose if struck and blown out immediately. The smell of tobacco smoke is in no way likely to frighten game, as, if a beast is able to detect it, it is equally certain that he will be able to wind the stalker. Personally, I use a pipe as a wind-finder more than anything else, and I have had a lighted pipe in my mouth at the time of firing at more than half of the game I have killed.

However, as Chapman reveals, spotting a lion, if even only metres from you, is no mean feat.

*At twenty yards' distance it seemed impossible that so
large a beast as a lion could still be lying in so small a bush
without my seeing it. They must, I thought, have slipped
away unobserved, and I was walking on almost carelessly
until within ten yards of the right-hand bush, when Elmi
suddenly seized my arm, pointing the rifle he carried
into the base of the bush, and hissed 'See! See! The lion!
Shoot – him spring.' Once more I must admit that I could
see nothing. Strain my eyes as I would I could distinguish
nothing like a lion in that bush – nothing beyond a very
small patch of monotone in the further corner. Yet Elmi
was so positive, and the bush so small and so near, that
I decided, rather recklessly – and perhaps from some
sense of shame that a black man should be so superior in
eyesight – to fire. There was no mistaking the response – a
growl more savage than ever I had heard in my life before.
I also saw, through the thick smoke from the Paradox*,
the electric convulsion with which the beast pulled itself
together for a spring. That movement disclosed the position
of the head and shoulder, and before there was any time
for mischief I got the second bullet well in behind the
shoulder. That knocked out any idea of a fight, and the
beast, still growling but mortally sick, crawled out beyond.*

* A Paradox was a gun developed by Holland & Holland that could
be used as a rifle or a shotgun. This type of gun was especially useful
for hunters in India and Africa who might encounter both large and
small prey on the same hunt.

As Chapman described, aiming at the correct spot on an
animal is vital if you are to ensure a swift and clean kill.
Rowland Ward's *Sportsman's Handbook* (1923) advises:

*To speak first of the members of the cat tribe, or Felidae,
the place to hit a lion, if you are quite sure of your aim,
as you may be if he is quiescent, is undoubtedly the brain.
In a lion, and similarly in a tiger, the brain is about the
size of an apple, and small in comparison to the size of
the skull, the brain-pan being situated about three or four
inches to the rear of the eye. The heart is also indicated,
and when the animal is broadside-on it can be pierced by
a shot behind the shoulder. When he is charging direct
towards you, the best shot to deliver is a little to the right or
left of the head, straight through the shoulder, for by this
you may pierce the heart, or possibly fracture the spinal
cord, while the bullet may traverse the body lengthwise
with paralysing effect, or it will – which is most important
– shatter the shoulder-bone and prevent the deadly spring.*

Incidentally …

*Rhinoceroses, on the other hand, are best killed by piercing
the brain, by fracturing the spinal column in the region of
the neck, or, less satisfactorily, by reaching the heart.*

… and indeed …

*Turning to the hippopotamus, it may be observed that if
these animals are fired at just as they rise to the surface
of the water, they should receive the bullet up the nostril,
as being the surest road to the brain. When stricken,
a hippopotamus sinks, and it may be an hour or two
before his body rises; the time depending greatly on the
temperature of the water.*

The lion being so disabled by at least three good shots, caution must still be advised, and sticks and stones should be thrown at the animal to ensure it is truly dead. R. Gordon Cumming notes in his 1850 book *A Hunter's Life in South Africa* that the Boers employed natives to throw sticks at an injured lion to see if it stirred. The hunters would not approach until an unfortunate boy had been selected to pull the lion by its tail, an action sure to reveal whether the beast still lived. Cumming provided the following cautionary tale.

On one of these occasions a Boer, who had dismounted from his horse to fire, was dashed to the ground by the lion before he could regain his saddle. The brute, however, did not injure him, but merely stood over him, lashing

*his tail, and growling at the rest of the party, who had
galloped to a distance in the utmost consternation, and,
instead of approaching within easy shot of the lion, to the
rescue of their comrade, opened their fire upon him from
a great distance, the consequence of which sportsmanlike
proceeding was, that they missed the lion, and shot their
comrade dead on the spot. The lion presently retreated,
and, none daring to follow him, he escaped.*

Fallen comrades notwithstanding, the hunt should end
with the lion categorically dead. The hunter may then take
his prize back to camp to begin the process of skinning
and mounting his trophy (see page 119).

How to afford introductions

The etiquette of introducing people to one another has
baffled hosts for centuries. Fortunately the Victorians
were very big on this sort of thing, and kindly created
some rules, which I have here extracted from the 1843
work *Etiquette for Gentlemen*.

*The inferior should be presented to the superior – I use the
terms in reference to personal distinction – a gentlemen to
a lady.*

*When two gentlemen of the same rank, &c., are
introduced to each other, perform the operation with
mathematical simplicity and precision, – 'Mr. A., Mr. B.;
Mr. B., Mr. A.'*

This all seems fairly self-explanatory and, dare I say, sensible. Indeed one can imagine applying these rules quite successfully at a work do, a summer barbecue or even an illegal rave. But then we get to the following ...

A gentleman should not be introduced to a lady without her permission being previously asked.

This brings a plethora of complications to any impromptu meeting, a fact which is further compounded by the next piece of advice.

If, in the course of a walk in company with a friend, you happen to meet, or are joined by an acquaintance, do not commit the too common, but most flagrant error, of introducing such persons to one another.

Having read this advice we go from sailing through social occasions without a care, to feeling that we have committed social suicide by introducing Bob to Dave whilst on a Sunday stroll.

How to pack for a 12-month expedition into the interior of Africa

Pioneers heading off into the African wilderness generally furnished themselves with a Cape wagon on which to transport their provisions and the many animal skins and trophies they hoped to accumulate. R Gordon Cumming, in his 1850 book *A Hunter's Life in South Africa*, listed the following goods to be taken on a 12-month-long expedition.

Two sacks containing 300 lbs of coffee, four quarter-chests of tea, 300 lbs sugar, 300 lbs rice, 180 lbs of meal, 100 lbs of flour, 5 lbs of pepper, 100 lbs of salt, an anker of vinegar, several large jars of pickles, half a dozen hams and cheeses, 2 cases of gin, 1 anker of brandy, 1 half-aum of Cape brandy, iron baking-pots with long legs, stewing and frying pans, saucepans and gridirons, tin water-buckets, of various sizes, 2 large 'fagie' or water-casks, an accompaniment which no Cape waggon is ever without, 2 large flasks of tar to be subsequently mixed with hard fat for greasing the wheels when required, 6 dozen pocket knives, 24 boxes of snuff, 50 lbs of tobacco, 300 lbs of white, coral, red and bright blue beads of various sizes; 3 dozen tinder-boxes, 1 cwt. of brass and copper wire, which the bechuana tribes, especially those dwelling to the east, readily barter and convert into ornaments for their legs and arms; 2 dozen sickles, 2 spades, 2 shovels, 1 pickaxe, 5 superior American axes, 2 augers, 1 stock and 36 bits, hatchets, planes, drawing knives, several coarse chisels for waggon-work, a vice, blacksmith and carpenters hammers, and a variety of other tools appertaining to both these professions. A gross of awls, a gross of sail-needles, 50 hanks of sail twine, 2 bolts of sail canvass, several rolls of stout woollen cloths, 2 dozen gown-pieces, 6 dozen Malay handkerchiefs; thread, needles and buttons; ready-made jackets and trowsers for my people, several dozen coarse shirts, Scotch bonnets and cocker-nonnys (as for shoes colonial servants are supposed to make them for themselves).

Additionally Cummings took wagons, oxen, horses, a tent, bedding, table and chair, plus a huge arsenal of guns and ammunition with which to dispatch the local wildlife.

How to make Stilton cheese

British Husbandry by John Burke (1834) contains the following recipe for making Stilton cheese, which could still be used today.

Stilton cheese which has become proverbial for its richness, was first made near Melton, in Leicestershire, by a relation of the landlord of the Old Bell Inn at Stilton, which gave the name.

It is made by putting the night's cream, without any portion of the skimmed milk, to the milk of the following morning; but those who wish to make it very fine, add a still greater quantity of cream, and of course the richness of the cheese depends upon the amount which is used. Butter is also said to be sometimes mixed with it. The rennet is then added without any colouring; and when the curd has come, it is taken out without being broken, and put whole into a sieve, or drainer, where it is pressed with weights until completely cleared of whey: when dry it is put, with a clean cloth, into a hooped chessart [the cheese-vat or container], and placed under the press, the outer coat being first salted. When sufficiently firm to be removed from this mould, the cheese is placed upon a dry board, and tightly bound in a cloth, which is changed daily in order to avoid all danger of cracks in the skin, until this is

MINNE.

found to be tolerably well coated; after which it is no longer used and the cheese requires no further care than being frequently turned upside down, and occasionally brushed.

The cheeses of this kind, although not much larger than the crown of a good sized hat — the form of which they much resemble — and not weighing more than about a dozen pounds, yet require nearly two years to bring them to perfect maturity, for they are not generally thought sufficiently mellowed for use until considerably decayed; and, in order to forward their ripeness, it is said that besides their being placed in damp, but warm, cellars, they are sometimes wrapped in strong brown paper, and sunk in a hot-bed.

We are also told that the flavour of an old cheese may be communicated to a new one of whatever species, by the insertion of some portions being intermixed with it. This is done by extracting small pieces with the sample-scoop from each cheese, and interchanging them; by which means the new one, if well covered up from the air, will in a few weeks become thoroughly impregnated with the mould, and with a flavour hardly to be distinguished from the old one.

How to look after your hair

The Handbook of the Toilette (1839) describes a woman's crowning glory thus:

One of the most admired ornaments of the person is the hair. So necessary is it considered to the perfection of female charms, that any loss or deterioration of this covering of the head impairs the beauty of women to such a degree that artificial locks are often added to those scantily furnished by nature, in order to give the proper effect to a set of beautiful features, which, without such aid, would be deprived of half their power.

While containing a wealth of advice for keeping the hair looking good, the book also includes a somewhat dubious description of the composition of hair.

The hair, according to the analysis of the most experienced chemists, is composed of various substances: 1. Animal matter; containing albumen and a very minute quantity of gelatine, in a hard form, as in the nails. 2. A white concrete oil, which maintains the hair in a glossy and supple condition: upon the proportion of this oil depends the smoothness or harshness of the hair. 3. Another oil, which gives the colour to the hair, and may therefore be termed its colouring principle. 4. A small quantity of iron. 5. A few particles of the protoxide of manganese. 6. A small portion of carbonate of lime. 7. A conspicuous quantity of silicic acid. 8. A very considerable quantity of sulphur. This latter substance varies in quantity in the hair of different persons. In some it is so great that, when the individual is heated, the smell of the sulphur in the hair is very perceptible.

From doubtful science we return to some helpful haircare advice.

The skin of the head must therefore be kept perfectly clean, and in a state of proper tone. To effect this, a brush should be used thrice a day if possible, which is strong, not too close, and will penetrate through the hair to the skin. This application of the brush, on rising in the morning, should last full half an hour; and if the hair belong to a lady, and be very thick and long, a quarter of an hour more should be devoted to brushing it, making it in all three quarters of an hour. On dressing for dinner, the brush should be applied to the head during five or six minutes, and during about ten minutes at night. It is often serviceable to rub into the hair in the morning, before the brush is applied, either hair-powder or bran, — it is almost immaterial which, though I think the first preferable.

There follows a word of warning for those seeking to dye their hair.

There are as many nostrums for dyeing the hair as for preventing or curing baldness. The inventor of Macassar oil composed a hair dye which he called 'Essence of Tyre'. This was only a solution of nitrate of silver (Lunar caustic). It would dye the hair first red; but by repeated applications, different shades were acquired until black was at last obtained. If, however, the hair, prior to the application of the Essence of Tyre, had been washed with a strong aqueous solution of carbonate of soda, and then allowed to dry without being wiped, a single application of the dye-liquid would have made the hair black; whilst by decomposing the nitrate of silver at the moment of its action, the carbonate of soda would have prevented the dye from injuring the substance of the hair. The use of Essence of Tyre was attended with several insurmountable defects: it dyed the skin as well as the hair; it blackened the fingers; it burnt the linen upon which it fell; and, what was worse than all, it destroyed the substance of the hair.

How to put back a dislocated jaw

Household Medicine and Surgery, Sick-room Management and Cookery for Invalids (1854) suggests, somewhat alarmingly, that a jaw may be easily dislocated.

The lower jaw is sometimes dislocated by gaping or yawning widely, or even by a very hearty laugh. The mouth is suddenly fixed, and wide open; the person cannot speak, and makes the strangest grimaces while endeavouring to do so.

Fortunately some simple advice to correct the problem soon follows.

It is for the most part easy to reduce. The thumbs, well-guarded by linen being wrapt round them, should be placed on the back part of the lower jaw, one thumb on each side. Firm pressure downwards is now to be made, while the chin is forced upwards with the fingers, or by an assistant. When it is felt that the bone is on the point of yielding, the thumbs should be slipped to the outside of the jaw so as to guard against every chance of their being bitten. Where no one will risk his fingers, the pressure may be made with the handle of a fork or a piece of wood.

How to read the future with snails

Ancient Legends, Mystic Charms, and Superstitions of Ireland by Lady Wilde (1887) suggests that the key to reading your future is to utilise the common or garden snail.

Another mode of divination for future fate in life is by snails. The young girls go out early before sunrise to trace the path of the snails in the clay, for always a letter is marked, and this is the initial of the true lover's name. A black snail is very unlucky to meet first in the morning, for his trail would read death; but a white snail brings good fortune.

How to make turnip wine

One would have thought the words turnips and wine should never be found together, and yet here they are. *A Shilling's Worth of Practical Receipts* (1856) contains the following recipe. Try it at your own risk.

Pare and slice what quantity of turnips you like, put them into a cyder press, and squeeze out what juice you can. To every gallon of juice put three pounds of lump sugar, put both into a vessel just large enough to hold them, and add to every gallon of juice half a pint of brandy. Lay something over the bung for a week, and when it has done working, bung it down close. Let it stand three months, then draw it off into another vessel, and when fine, put into bottles.

How to bandage an arm

With the relentless rise of Tubigrip, few people now have the skills to tie a proper bandage. Here *Cassell's Home Encyclopedia* (1934) describes a suitably elaborate method for bandaging an injured hand and arm.

With the arm and hand palm downwards, the bandage is laid across the back of the wrist, the free end towards the patient's body, and kept in position by the operator's free hand. The roll is then carried across the back of the hand from thumb side to little finger side, around the outer side, across under the palm, up through the angle between the thumb and first finger, over the back of the hand, around the wrist and again over the back of the hand from the thumb side towards the little finger side.

Two or three of these figure of eight loops will cover the hand. A spiral bandage is then continued up the arm, the spiral being reversed when necessary. At the elbow a return may be made to the figure of eight turns, similar to those described above.

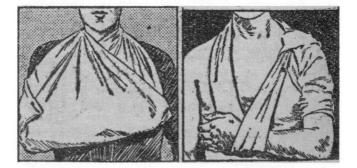

How to travel across the desert without water

R. Gordon Cumming describes in his 1850 book *A Hunter's Life in South Africa* a technique used by Bushmen to make daring raids on the Boer farmers who had settled the region. The Bushmen would steal cattle and then make good their escape across the great expanse of desert, safe in the knowledge that their superior bush skills would mean the pursuing Boers could not hope to catch them.

As the Bushmen travelled on foot they had to find a way to outsmart the Boer farmers pursuing them by horseback. The Bushmen used the lack of fresh water in the desert to ensure their advantage, waiting until the hottest, driest season to attack. Cumming reports that the Bushman circumvented this problem themselves in the following fashion.

They had regular stages at long intervals in a direct-line across the desert, where, assisted by their wives, they concealed water in ostrich-eggs, which they brought from amazing distances, and these spots, being marked by some slight inequality in the ground, they could discover either by day or night from their perfect knowledge of the country. They were thus able to fearlessly drive off a herd of cattle, whose sufferings from thirst gave them little concern and to travel day and night, while their mounted pursuers, requiring light to hold the spoor, could necessarily only follow by day, and were soon obliged to give up the pursuit on account of their horses being without water.

This technique would, of course, require meticulous planning, a large number of ostrich eggs and the ability to navigate a seemingly never-ending and apparently featureless landscape – which may discourage modern readers from employing the method.

How to preserve food

Remember it is all to your benefit to preserve because:
You save fruit and vegetables etc., which would be wasted at a glut period.
You provide yourselves with cheap and excellent foods during a period when such foods are expensive or unobtainable.
You improve your health and that of your family.
You find an added interest in life and an absorbing hobby, and
You help to reduce the volume of imports into this country and so assist the Nation's finances.

So writes Cyril Grange in his 1949 paean to preservation, *The Complete Book of Home Food Preservation*. Grange goes on to detail his ten methods for preserving food, noting the following.

Preserving merely consists of a) killing the moulds, yeasts and bacteria, b) maintaining a condition in which these factors cannot exert an ill influence or sealing the product so that an influx of fresh moulds, etc., is made impossible. The ten methods are:

By heating – bottling and canning.
By drying – dried fruit and vegetables.
By salting – salted fruits and vegetables.
By freezing – fruits and vegetables.
By the use of vinegar – pickles, chutneys, sauces, ketchups.
By the use of sulphur dioxide – fruits only with Campden
tablets, sulphurous acid and calcium bisulphite.
By the use of sugar – jams, marmalades, jellies, curds,
conserves, preserves, pastes, cheeses, butters, syrups and
candied fruits.
By the use of chemicals – fruit syrups (sodium benzoate).
By the production of alcohol – wines and ciders.
By the production of vinegar – fruit vinegars.

One of the mostly widely and usefully preserved foodstuffs is fruit. Before bottling a glut of plums, Grange recommends that you first remove their skins, and he provides two methods for doing so.

The Hot Water Dip Method: The simplest plan is to gather up the fruit in a butter-muslin bag and hold in boiling water for 20–60 seconds according to variety. Then take out and cool as quickly as possible in a large basin of cold water. The skins can then be peeled off with a knife or slipped off with the fingers.

The Caustic Soda Method: This method is much used in America and is valuable when large quantities of fruit are to be peeled, but should not be used for very ripe or soft fruit. The exact instructions must be followed. The action of the caustic is to dissolve the skin without injuring the flesh beneath. A 1.3 per cent solution is prepared by dissolving four tablespoonfuls of caustic soda in one gallon of cold water and bringing to boiling point. Never add water to the caustic; always caustic to the water. Use a stick for stirring and keep solution away from your flesh or clothes. The solution may be rather stronger and the period of immersion longer for the hard skinned green fruit, and weaker for the soft ripe ones.

The procedure is: 1) place the fruit in a metal or woven wire basket, 2) dip in hot water for 10 seconds, 3) into the boiling caustic for 20 seconds, 4) then into boiling water in which they are agitated for 20 seconds, and 5) finally washing off all traces of caustic beneath the tap of cold water. The skin falls away on washing and leaves the flesh unimpaired.

The skins of the fruit removed, Grange goes on to describe the process of bottling the fruit.

The operations described below appertain to all descriptions of fruit bottling ... The purpose is the same, namely to kill all moulds, yeasts and bacteria and then to seal so that decomposition is made impossible.
The sequence of operations for all methods, every one of which must be properly carried out, are:
Providing, cleaning and testing the bottles.
Selecting and preparing the fruit.
Packing into the bottles.
Preparing the covering liquid.
Filling the bottles.
Adjusting the caps.
Sterilizing by a) hot water, b) dry heat or c) chemical means.
Sealing down and allowing to cool (12 hours minimum).
Testing for sealing.
Storing away.

Should the reader become confused as to what to do with the fruits of their preserving labour, Grange helpfully adds a final step.

Using.

How to keep cigars

Any fool knows how to keep cigars, you may think, and yet as *Cassell's Home Encyclopedia* (1934) points out: 'The proper keeping of cigars is important.' The encyclopedia goes on to issue the following recommendations.

Choice tobacco leaf is extremely sensitive to atmosphere and to odours in the atmosphere, and will readily absorb them and affect its own taste. Paint, for instance, and especially wet paint, will ruin any cigar or tobacco placed near it. Salt sea-air will completely spoil a fine cigar. Therefore cigars must be kept in airtight boxes. Cedar-wood is the best material for the box.

So there you have it: under no circumstance leave your best Havanas out while the decorator visits, nor allow your cigars a trip to the seaside.

How a lady should conduct herself in polite society

Some advice is timeless, as we can see from the gems imparted by *Etiquette for the Ladies – Eighty Maxims on Dress, Manners and Accomplishments* (1838).

If you are a married lady, and have children, never insist on showing off their precocity before company. In nine cases out of ten, however much people may affect to applaud, depend upon it they look upon such exhibitions as a bore.

Never allow your pursuit after fashion to be so eager, as to make people suppose that you have nothing better than the mode of your dress to recommend you.

Perfumes are not altogether to be forbidden; but they should never be so strong or in such quantity, as to excite attention. When they are used too profusely, people are apt to suppose that you have some particular reason for their use, beyond the mere desire to gratify your olfactory organ.

Other nuggets of advice contained in this august publication have not stood the test of time so well.

It is not considered proper for ladies to wear gloves during dinner. To appear in public without them – to sit in church or in a place of public amusement destitute of these appendages, is decidedly vulgar. Some gentlemen insist on stripping off their gloves before shaking hands; – a piece of barbarity, of which no lady will be guilty.

Coloured shoes are not considered consistent with good taste, though delicate pink and faint blue silk each have their advocates. White satin, or black satin or kid, and bronze kid, will be found to afford sufficient variety to harmonize with all dresses.

Scarcely any thing is so repulsive in a lady – so utterly plebeian, as speaking in a loud harsh voice. As in Shakespeare's time, a 'small' voice is still considered 'an excellent thing in a woman.'

How to break a horse

Horse breaking was a great skill; it took much patience and experience to ensure that the horse was calmly and systematically tamed. Robert Moreton, in his 1883 work *On Horse Breaking*, first shares his advice for how *not* to break in a horse.

The first step towards the breaking-in of a horse is placing a halter upon his head … There are many methods of doing this in vogue, most of which are by brute force; for instance, a farmer has a colt he wishes to halter, so he gets his men together, and drives the colt into a yard or stable; a man then hangs on to the timid animal by one of his ears and his nose, another man seizes his tail, whilst three or four men push against either side of the poor frightened beast; then ensues a struggle: the colt, frightened out of his senses and not knowing what is required of him, fights the half-dozen men clinging to him; he rears, kicks, bites, and strikes with his fore feet. The men on seeing this, and the farmer standing near, aye he is a savage brute, and must be reduced by savage means. The colt is then beaten with a broom or pitchfork-handle, his tail is twisted, and every means of inflicting excruciating pain is resorted to, which, instead of subduing the animal has the reverse effect; the colt, being driven to madness, struggles and fights until he vanquishes his foes. There is then a consultation between the farmer and his men, and at last this ferocious beast is haltered by stratagem, but throughout all his life he is either vicious or extremely nervous and shy, for he will never forget his first introduction to mankind, and the rough usage he then underwent.

Moreton goes on to explain the correct way to halter a horse.

The colt or filly to be haltered should be driven into a yard,
stable or loose box as quietly as possible – the best way
being to lead an old horse, and endeavour to entice the
young one to follow ... After the removal of the old horse,
and the stable door being closed, one man only should be
in the stable with the colt, who will endeavour to get him
into the loose box, the door of which should have been
previously opened ... the man in the stable must keep quiet,
and allow the colt to smell about and inspect everything ...
the great thing is time; take plenty of time ... By degrees
the colt gets nearer his loose box, and out of sheer curiosity
walks in to inspect it. Now is your time; walk up quickly
but quietly and close the door ... You had better now leave

*the colt alone for half an hour or so, so that he may become
accustomed to his new quarters.*

*Select a halter with a long 'shank' and tie a knot in it
so as to prevent the nose-band pinching on the jaws when
the colt pulls at the rope on finding he is fast. Enter the
loose box and close the door, hang the halter up out of
the way of the colt, for it is better to approach him first
without it. Avoid all unnecessary movements of the arms,
as they will frighten the colt; when you do take a step, do it
slowly and quietly; if you only take one step in a minute,
it will repay you; be deliberate, quiet and gentle in every
movement. The colt will now be watching you, not being
able to understand what is going to happen. Speak to him
soothingly, and approach gently and slowly. Watch him,
do not stare at his eyes with a ferocious look, as people do,
under the impression that by so doing they can subdue the
wildest animal.*

*Some colts will allow you to touch their heads directly,
whilst others – and I think they are the most numerous
– present their tails to you. Anyhow, in whichever part they
seem most inclined to allow your first caresses, you must make
it your rule to, by degrees, manipulate towards the head.*

*Now that the colt has allowed you to handle him to a
certain extent, and has found you are not going to hurt
him, you may leave his side (quietly and slowly as you
approached him) and get the halter you previously hung
up; but avoid all hurry, jerking the arm, etc. Hold the
halter in the left hand with the 'shank' coiled up, the end of
which you must grasp with the right hand. Approach the
colt gently as before, speaking soothingly to him ... having
reached the mane, pay the rope out slowly between your*

*fingers, so that it will fall on the off side of the neck; when
about eighteen inches to a couple of feet have been worked
out through your fingers, you will see the end of the rope
hanging down under the neck on the off side. You must
now keep handling the neck downwards until your hand
is close to the rope's end, when you must catch it quietly
and tie it on the near side so as to form a noose round the
animal's neck.*

*The next move is to endeavour to place the halter on his
head with your left hand, whilst you hold the rope in your
right, thus having partial control over the animal. When
the halter is near his nose he will 'bob' his head, move away
and feeling the constraint of the rope around his neck for
the first time, will struggle and endeavour to drag you to
the other side of the box; but he will soon give in, and then
you can easily place the halter on his head, after which
untie the 'shank' round his neck, and all is finished.
If you can spare time, after placing the head-stall on the
colt's head you may handle him for a time, then place
water and food within his reach, and leave him to himself
for the rest of the day to get accustomed to his new headdress.*

Once that first battle is won and the horse has the halter
in place, the task of training the beast may begin.

*On the following day you can handle him quietly in the
loose box, and offer him choice locks of hay or corn out of
your hand to increase his intimacy with you, and then you
may tie a rope to his head-stall and fasten him up. He is
sure to struggle when he finds himself tied up, therefore
you must not leave him; for if you have done your work*

*properly he will have already recognised you as a friend
and not a foe, and will, when he hears you speaking to him
soothingly and encouragingly, become quieter by degrees,
and will soon cease to resist.*

So begins a long and steady process where the horse is
gently introduced to each piece of equipment (bridle,
saddle, stirrups etc.) and each day exercised a little,
interspersed with petting, chatting and patting to deepen
the connection between the rider and the horse. The horse
may be gently schooled to walk, trot or canter in circles
around the rider, attached as they are to a long rope on
their bridle. Build up until the horse is familiar with the
bridle and saddle and will happily circle the rider and stop
when commanded. The rider may then try to mount the
horse for the first time.

*Gathering up the reins in your left hand, and standing
with your left side to his shoulder, place your left foot in
the stirrup, and gradually bear weight upon it, when after
a while you may raise yourself in the stirrup, so that both
your legs are off the ground. You must watch minutely
every movement of the animal, and speak gently and
soothingly to him. After standing in the stirrups for a few
seconds, lower yourself to the ground again, and then
repeat the same a few times, until the colt seems quite
used to it, when you may throw your right leg gently over
his back, taking great care not to touch him with it, and
placing all your weight on your right hand ... When your
leg is over his back, gently lower it quietly into its proper
position, but keep from touching the animal's side until you*

have gently seated yourself in the saddle, then put your
foot in the stirrup, and there you are. Now do not spoil
things by trying to make the colt progress, but sit still, talk
to him, pat him, and do everything you can to pacify the
animal and get him used to seeing you take such liberties
with him as sitting on his back.

Moreton reveals the dedication and patience it takes to break a horse, a skill still practised today with similar techniques to those described here from over a hundred years ago.

How to use leeches

Leeches have been used medicinally for thousands of years as a way to bleed a patient and balance the humours. *Household Medicine and Surgery, Sick-room Management and Cookery for Invalids* (1854) recommends using the following leech.

The leech used for medical purposes is called the Hirudo
medicinalis, to distinguish it from other varieties, such as
the H. sanguisuga or horse-leech, and the H. provincialis,
or Lisbon leech. It varies from 2 to 4 inches in length and
is of a blackish brown colour, marked on the back with six
yellow spots, and edged with a yellow line on each side.

Once the correct leeches have been identified and collected for use, the patient must then be prepared for treatment.

When leeches are applied to a part, it should be thoroughly freed from down or hair by shaving, and all dirt, liniments, &c. carefully and effectually cleaned away by washing. If the leech is hungry it will soon bite; but sometimes great difficulty is experienced in getting the animal to fasten. When this is the case, roll the leech in a little porter, or moisten the surface with a little blood or milk, or sugar or water. Leeches may be applied by holding them over the part with a piece of linen cloth or by the means of a glass.

Caution is advised if using the leeches in sensitive areas.

When applied to the gums, care should be taken to use a leech glass, as they are apt to creep down the patient's throat; a large swan's quill will answer the purpose of a leech glass.

Once treatment is finished, the leeches must be removed.

When leeches are gorged, they will drop off themselves; never tear them off from a person, but just dip the tip of a moistened finger in some salt and touch them with that.

How to wear mourning

The Victorians were particularly keen on elaborate mourning rituals, encompassing special clothing, behaviour and strict rules relating to the amount of time spent mourning the dead. *Notices Historical and Miscellaneous Concerning Mourning Apparel* (1850) includes a description of the different colours worn for mourning.

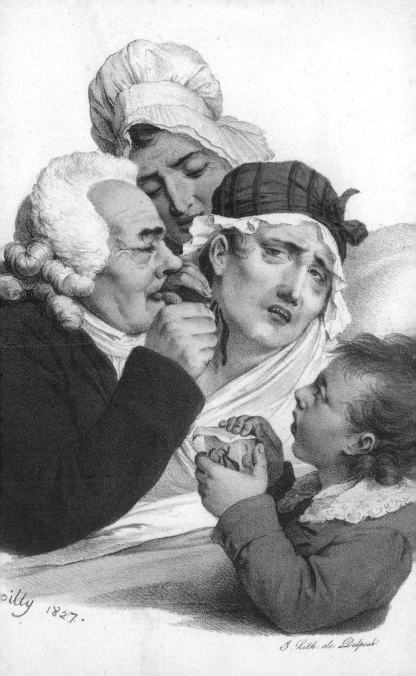

Billy 1827.

Lith. de Delpech

*The modes of mourning are various in various countries;
as are also the colours that obtain for that end. Throughout
Europe the ordinary colour for mourning is black; in
China, it is white; in Turkey, blue or violet; in Ethiopia,
brown. White prevailed formerly in Castile, on the death
of their princes … Each people pretend to have their
reasons for the particular colour of their mourning: white
is supposed to denote purity; yellow, that death is the end
of human hopes, in regard that leaves when they fall, and
flowers when they fade, become yellow; brown denotes the
earth, whither the dead return; black, the privation of life,
as being the privation of light; blue expresses the happiness
which it is hoped the deceased does enjoy; and purple or
violet, sorrow on one side, and hope on the other, as being a
mixture of black and blue.*

Incidentally, the author goes on to note the following.

*The pope's nieces never wear mourning, not even for
their nearest relations, as the Romans esteem it so great a
happiness to have a pope in the family, that nothing ought
to afflict his Holiness' kindred.*

The book also includes a fascinating glimpse into the
vagaries of Court mourning.

*The official orders for the regulation of Court mourning
which were issued, as occasion called, after the accession
of the House of Brunswick to the throne of these realms,
in 1714, continue up to this day to bear much of the same
form and aspect as they did a century ago. The following*

announcement is that which appeared in the London Gazette on the death of the Queen of Hanover, who was aunt to our reigning Sovereign, which event took place on the 29th June, 1841: –

Lord Chamberlain's Office, July 6th. Orders for the Court's going into Mourning, on Thursday next, the 8th instant, for her late Majesty the Queen of Hanover, aunt to the Queen – viz:

The Ladies to wear black silk. Fringed or plain linen, white gloves, necklaces and ear-rings, black or white shoes, fans and tippets.

The Gentlemen to wear black, full trimmed, fringed or plain linen, black swords and buckles.

The Court to change the mourning on Thursday, the 22nd instant – viz:

The ladies to wear black silk or velvet, coloured ribbons, fans, and tippets, or plain white, or white and gold, or white and silver stuffs, with black ribbons.

The Gentlemen to wear black coats, and black or plain white, or white and gold, or white and silver stuff of waistcoats, full trimmed, coloured swords and buckles.

And on Thursday, the 29th instant, the Court to go out of mourning.

A History of Mourning by Richard Davey (1889) contains information on how long mourning should continue, depending on the status of the dead person.

The following are regulations for Court mourning, according to the register at the Lord Chamberlain's office: –
For the King or Queen – full mourning, eight weeks,

mourning, two weeks; and half-mourning, two weeks: in
all, three full months.

For the son or daughter of the Sovereign – full
mourning, four weeks; mourning, one week; and half-
mourning, one week: total, six weeks.

For the brother or sister of the Sovereign – full
mourning, two weeks; mourning, four days; and half-
mourning, two days: total, three weeks.

Nephew or niece – full mourning, one week; half-
mourning, one week: total, two weeks.

Uncle or aunt – same as above.

Cousin, ten days; second cousin, seven days.

By providing such strict rules on mourning, the Victorians sought to standardise grief and therefore prevent any unnecessary emotion from seeping out. Unfortunately officially ending the mourning period does not signal the end of grief, as Queen Victoria herself attested to by wearing mourning for her late husband for the rest of her days.

How to carve meat

Carving the Sunday roast is a task that even in 1877 was not given its proper care and attention, as revealed in *Household Management* by 'An Old Housekeeper' (1877).

In the present day the art of carving is much neglected,
although it is so important to the comfort of every family,
and the economy of its expenditure; for, by properly

carving a joint, we may not only satisfy the choice of every one of the party, but leave the meat more fit to appear on the table a second time.

Fortunately, a series of tips to ensure successful carving is included.

There are certain conditions requisite to insure neat Carving. The knife should be sharp, not too heavy and of middling size.

The article to be carved should be placed in a dish sufficiently large to allow the joint to be turned; it should likewise be set firmly on the table, so near to the carver as to allow the plates between him and the dish.

Loins, breasts and necks of mutton, lamb and veal should be properly divided, or jointed, before they are dressed, else the most adroit carver will be baffled.

In carving and helping the joint, do not load a person's plate. If the meat is attached to a bone by too much, a slice may be cut from the meat of two bones.

In carving beef and mutton joints, cut the meat to the bone. The more solid joints, as a round of beef, or fillet of veal, should be cut in thin, even slices; as should also ham.

The more obvious cuts of meat there dealt with, the author goes on to recommend the best method for tackling those more tricky delights, such as a calf's head.

Calf's head should be cut lengthwise, from the nose to the neck, passing the knife through the flesh under the eye, quite to the bone. The throat sweetbread lies in the thick part of the neck-end, short slices of which may be served with the former. The most delicate part of a calf's head are the bit under the ears, next the eyes, and the side next the cheek. The tongue and brains are served in a separate dish.

How to see your future husband in a dream

For those finding the perils of internet dating too much like hard work, *The Book of Charms and Ceremonies: whereby all may have the opportunity of obtaining any object they desire* by 'Merlin' (1892) provides the following mystical advice to help you save yourself from the dating scene.

On St Andrew's Eve, a girl must take from a widow, and without returning thanks for it, an apple, and cut it in two, and must eat one half of it before midnight, and the other half after it; then in sleep she will see her future husband.

How to cure a headache

A New Herball by William Turner (1551) advised the following remedy for a headache.

To ease a man of the head ache, thus make his nose bleed: take seeds of red nettles and make them to a powder in a morter and blow a little of the same into his nose with a quill.

But if ye cannot get seeds of nettle *put a whole of a herbe called* milkfoyl *or* barbe *into the nose and rub the nose outward softly; then it should bleed. But if it be winter and ye cannot get nettles, etc., and would glad ease the head ache, then take two sack bands and tye them, first, firmly about the legs around the knees, and this for the space of half a pater noster. Then lose it again and tye it again.*

Do this the space of a quarter of an hour, then tye his arms about the elbow, likewise, thus shalt though draw the blood from his head. This must be done carefully lest his limbs become blue.

How to fashion an elephant's foot into something useful

A common source of trouble to the sportsman in Africa, India, Ceylon, etc., is the proper treatment of an elephant's foot. This part, as well as the head, is a recognised trophy,

*since it affords a gauge of the height of the animal, and
also because in ordinary circumstances the skin of this
mighty beast is so difficult to transport; and although it can
be converted into innumerable articles of domestic utility,
its value is by no means always appreciated. In the case
of the foot there are, however, no such difficulties, and it
is particularly suitable for conversion into useful articles,
without impairing its natural form and structure.*

So says Rowland Ward in his *Sportsman's Handbook*
(1923). Charles McCann in his *A Shikari's Pocket-book*
(1927) recommends that 'the feet of elephants may be
turned into useful trophies, such as stools or waste paper
baskets.' Ward then goes on to describe the method.

*The fore-foot should be severed either at the so-called knee
(that is, wrist) or at least 12 inches from the ground, and
a cut can be made, if necessary, down the back side; after
which the skin must be separated from the flesh. Remove
every particle of flesh, because if any is left it is liable
to get tainted, when it will be impossible to get rid of the
odour. If possible, wash the inside of the skin with carbolic
water, or apply powdered preservative both inside and
outside. Then place the foot to dry in the shade, taking care
that the skin does not fold and is in all parts accessible to the
air. Although not absolutely necessary, it is desirable that
the skin should dry in the natural shape. It is a good plan
to insert a big bottle or block of wood in the centre, round
which dry sand may be rammed, so as to distend the skin
as nearly as possible to the natural shape.*

On a roll now, of tips for turning once-majestic beasts into useful bits of household hardware, Ward imparts the following advice.

The shields or plates of a rhinoceros — the thick portions of the hides between the folds — should be brought away entire, and can be made into table-tops, trays, boxes, inkstands, sticks, whips, etc., which, if kept dry and free from undue heat and damp, will retain their shape.

How to keep fresh breath

The horrors of bad breath are described and remedies recommended in *The Handbook of the Toilette* (1839).

If ladies were conscious of the effect produced upon the breath by late hours, heating diet, hot and crowded rooms, and the several other enemies to the constitution necessarily encountered by a life of dissipation, they would be horror-stricken at finding that they render themselves offensive and disgusting to those whom it is their duty as well as their best policy to please. The same remark applies to men under similar circumstances, joined perhaps to a habit of taking wine and ardent spirits, if not to excess, at least in greater quantity than is requisite. In the morning the body is feverish, the tongue loaded with a white crust; vapours rise from the stomach, and the breath is foul. And when this mode of life is continued, in addition to the loss of the bloom given by health, the breath is most offensively impregnated with fetid exhalations from the stomach.

The most effective sweetener of the breath is health of body, which can be obtained by the means I have already pointed out; but where vapours and fermentation of the stomach exist, the only substances which can destroy the fetid exhalations, are the disinfecting chlorides. All perfumes used to wash the mouth, catechu [extract of the Acacia tree], *musk, ambergris, mastic, orris-root, or other substances chewed, do no more than combine their powerful odours with the fetor that exhales from the stomach, causing a sickly compound often more intolerable than the stench itself freed from the perfume.*

As the solution of chloride of lime is too harsh, the concentrated solution of the chloride of soda ... should alone be admitted at the toilette. From six to ten drops of this substance in a wineglassful of pure spring water, taken immediately after the operations of the morning are completed, will instantly sweeten the breath, by disinfecting the stomach, which, far from being injured, will be benefitted by the medicine.

How to remove freckles

In the Victorian era freckles were seen as blemishes. This was probably because they were associated with the lower classes, who were more likely to be exposed to the sun while working outside. The Victorian ideal was pale, white skin, and to achieve this *A Shilling's Worth of Practical Receipts* (1856) recommended the following tip to banish freckles.

*Take tincture of benzoin, 1 pint; tincture of totu, half a pint;
oil of rosemary, quarter of an ounce. Mix. One tea-spoonful
of the tincture to be put in half a gill of water, and with a
towel dipped in this, rub well the face night and morning.*

How to survive without a fridge

*How the Anglo-Indians in former times managed to get
on without ice, and how those who live on the plains of the
mofussil still do so, is a puzzle to those within easy reach
of the icehouses today, who have come to regard it as a
positive necessary of life, and who bewail the hardship
should the supply now and then fall short for a few weeks.
Every household in the towns where it is kept (except
perhaps some of them for a month or two during the cool
season) consumes several pounds of ice daily, a glass of
water being seldom taken without a lump having been put
in to cool it; while wine and beer are kept in the ice box for
the same purpose.*

So wrote Edmund C.P. Hull in *The European in India*
(1874). Hull goes some way to describe the importance
and luxury afforded by ice, something that we today find
hard to imagine because of the ubiquity of the fridge-
freezer. Andrew Wynter in his 1866 title *Our Social Bees*
describes what he might say to a child who asks where the
ice in his glass came from.

*A very long way off, in the New World, there is a great
cup, hundreds of feet deep, made in the mountains. This*

cup is always full of crystal water, which in the winter
season gets so cold that great ships come and carry it all
over the world, so that every person, when he is heated as
you are, can, if he likes, have a draught of its delicious icy
contents.

In all probability the child would probably think we
were telling it some tale of Fairyland, and would not
dream we were speaking of an everyday working fact.
Yet such is the case: the crystal cup is the Wenham Lake,
held in a hollow of the mountains in New Hampshire,
Massachusetts. This lake, which is of small extent, having
only an area of 500 acres, is supplied by springs which
issue from its rocky bottom: its waters are so pure that
analysis cannot detect any foreign elements held either in
suspension or in combination.

Wynter goes on to explain how the ice farms of the
nineteenth century furnished Europeans with enough ice
to keep their drinks cool all summer.

The condition of purity is not alone, however, the cause
of the celebrity which the ice formed from it has of late
years attained throughout the world, and especially in
England: there are many such lakes in America capable
of producing equally good ice, and which are indeed
used as the ice farms, if we may so term them, for home
consumption: the real reason of the celebrity of the ice
produced from the Wenham Lake lies in the fact of it
being near the seaboard, which enables the company to
which it belongs to ship it easily to all parts of the world.
This lake is only eighteen miles north-east of Boston, and

*by means of the Eastern Railway, which receives a branch
line from the lake itself, is within an hour's run of the
wharf at that city; so that, for all practical purposes, the ice
might be said to be formed at the ship's side.*

*The ice trade in America has long since reached
a magnitude of which we in the old country have no
conception ... The Americans consume pretty much the
same quantity of ice in the winter as in the summer. With
every meal it is placed upon the table, and it forms a
constituent of all their drinks. In England, a publican will
tell you that two-thirds of his spirit-drinking customers
will call for hot brandy-and-water; in an American liquor-
store, the constant demand is for a glass of sherry with a
knob of ice in it, or cocktail, or mint julep, with the like
accompaniment of liquefying crystal.*

*The aggregate consumption of this article throughout
the States must be something enormous, for in Boston
alone upwards of 50,000 tons are consumed annually – a
much larger quantity than is used throughout England.
The ice-crop of America is consequently of great national
importance; and as it is liable to perish by change of
weather, even more quickly than grain, human ingenuity
has been brought into play to cut and house it with a speed
and regularity strongly contrasting with the rude manner
of smashing it with poles and shovelling in the irregular
lumps, such as we see practised upon our home-grown ice.*

Wynter then goes on to describe how the ice was harvested.

*Operations are begun by ruling a line as it were across the
slippery surface of a circumscribed space of about three*

or four acres; this line is made by a small and exceedingly sharp hand-plough, which cuts along the solid mass, throwing up as it progresses a glittering dust. This line, which is two or three inches in depth, serves as a guide to a machine drawn by horses, called the marker, which traversing beside it, cuts two parallel lines, about twenty-one inches apart. Similar lines are drawn until the whole surface is thus marked. The grooves are now deepened to six inches by the action of a horse-plough. A similar process is carried on at right angles; so that when the whole is finished, the entire area is divided into squares of twenty-one inches each way.

The next step is to detach these blocks from each other, and lift them out of the water. To accomplish this a saw is brought into play, and a line of squares having been cut through, the remainder are easily detached and floated out by means of the ice spade, a wedge-like implement, which no sooner enters the groove, than the block splits off with the utmost ease – that is provided the weather is frosty during the operation; otherwise the task is not quite so easy, the ice being much more tough when thawing. The floating squares are now to be secured and housed; for this purpose, a low platform is placed near the edge of the ice, having an inclined plane of iron, which dips down into the water. Up this plane the great blocks are jerked by the ice-man, who wields his ice-hook with great dexterity. When a load is secured, it is transferred to a sledge, and drawn to the ice stores which line one side of the lake.

The ice-houses are themselves worthy of attention; built of pine-wood, with double walls, placed about two feet *apart, the space being filled up with sawdust, a very perfect non-conducting material.*

When the ice is wanted either for home consumption or shipment, it is placed in air-tight trucks, which carry it at once along the line to Boston, and even to the ship's side. When taken on board, it is carefully packed in sawdust, and excluded as much as possible from external salt air. But, notwithstanding every precaution that it is possible to take, waste of from a third to a half of its substance often occurs.

Arrived in this country, it is stored in the warehouses belonging to the company. These are situated in the dry arches supporting the waterloo-road, which, towards the bridge, are at least forty feet high and seventy feet long … The visitor who is curious enough to inspect these storehouses sees nothing but huge heaps of sawdust: but the frosty breath issuing from his mouth makes him aware of the low temperature of the atmosphere. In the season, as much as two thousand tons of ice are sometimes stored here without losing much in weight.

This evocative description of the great process to harvest and store ice serves to remind us how far we have come in modern life, where nearly everyone seeking ice just needs to wander into their kitchen and open the freezer. Yet somehow that doesn't quite have the magic of cooling your drink with a chunk of American lake ice which has travelled thousands of miles over land and sea.

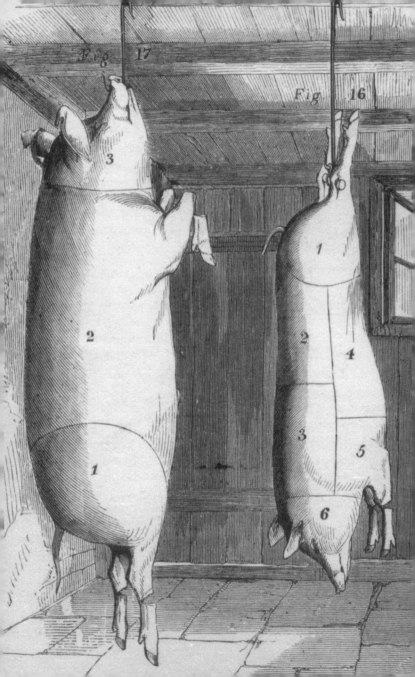

Fig. 17

Fig. 16

How to smoke your own bacon

The Art and Mystery of Curing, Preserving, and Potting all Kinds of Meats, Game, and Fish (1864) records the following method for smoking your own bacon.

Take a side or 'middle' of dairy-fed pork from a pig not exceeding eight score pounds weight, and mixing well: —

Bay or rock salt, pounded	*1 ½ lb*
Coarse sugar	*1 lb*
Shallots, minced	*1 oz.*
Saltpetre*, in powder	*1 oz.*
Sal prunelle**, in powder	*1 oz.*
Bay leaves	*2 oz.*

Rub both sides of the meat well for a week, turning it every other day, then add common salt and treacle, each one pound, and rub again daily for a week; after which baste and turn only, for a week longer, then take it up, dry with coarse cloths, rub it well all over with peas meal and bran mixed, equal quantities, and hang it to be smoked with: —

Oak lops or sawdust	*2 parts*
Dried fern	*2 parts*
Peat or bog-earth	*2 parts*

For three weeks. Commit it to your ham and bacon chest, to be kept three months or longer, well embedded in malt coom*** and pulverised charcoal. It will never be rancid.

---

* Saltpetre is potassium nitrate, a compound with many uses from food preservation to gunpowder. It is not so commonly used in food these days as it is not as reliable as other nitrates, but where it is used in the EU it is listed as the 'E number' E252.

** Nitrate of potash fused together and cast into round moulds so as to look like little plums (or prunelles).
*** The withered rootlets of malt.

How to perform cupping

These days cupping is the preserve of the Hollywood health fanatic, but as *Household Medicine and Surgery, Sick-room Management and Cookery for Invalids* (1854) describes, it was used by the Victorians to cure many ills.

Cupping is performed by throwing a piece of paper dipped into spirit of wine and ignited into a wine-glass and placing it over the part, such as the neck, temples &c. This is dry cupping. It draws flesh into the glass, and causes a determination of blood to the part, which is useful in headaches, or many other complaints. This is an excellent method of extracting the poison from wounds made by adders, mad dogs, fish, &c.

A further method, to increase blood flow, is also detailed.

Ordinary cupping is performed the same as dry cupping, with this exception, that the part is scarified or scratched with a lancet, so as to cause the blood to flow. Then the glass is placed over it again with the lighted paper in it, and when sufficient blood has been taken away, then the parts are sponged, and a piece of sticking plaster applied over them.

Fig. II.

How to get rid of fleas

Most will agree that fleas are an absolute nuisance and a flea infestation in the home is especially troublesome. Edmund C.P. Hull in *The European in India* (1874) offers up a somewhat foolhardy method to drive the blight from a house.

Fleas are undoubtedly one of the plagues of India. Houses that have been recently vacated become filled in an incredibly short time, and person entering will in a few minutes find themselves almost black with swarms of these vermin … To free empty houses of these insects, I have heard of resort being had to two curious expedients, which I may mention, but neither of which I can recommend: – (1) Putting a layer of straw over the whole floor of the house, and then setting it (the straw) alight; and (2) driving a herd of cattle through the building, to carry the fleas with them on their exit. In the first case, however, the house will probably be burned down; and in the second, damaged, without any effectual remedy being obtained for the evil complained of.

How to visit like a Victorian gentlemen

The Victorians created a plethora of rules surrounding paying a visit, which were further complicated by the tradition of leaving a visiting card. *Etiquette for Gentlemen* (1843) neatly sums up how to approach this minefield.

*In paying a visit under ordinary circumstances you leave
a single [visiting] card. If there be residing in the family,
a married daughter, an unmarried sister, a transient guest,
or any person in a distinct situation from the mistress of
the house, you leave two cards, one for each party. If you
are acquainted with only one member of a family, as the
husband, or the wife, and you wish to indicate that your
visit is to both, you leave two cards.*

*A visit and an umbrella should always be returned. In
returning a visit, however, it is not necessary to present
yourself personally – to leave a card is considered sufficient.*

More detail on the etiquette of visiting is offered by
*Complete Etiquette for Ladies and Gentlemen: A Guide to
the Rules and Observances of Good Society* (1900).

*First visits, that is to say calls commencing an acquaintance,
are always paid by the person of highest rank or social
consideration, and it is a solecism of etiquette for the lower
to make the first move, the exception being in the country,
where old residents call first on a newcomer.*

*A first visit, in London especially, is usually
accomplished by merely leaving cards, and when such
is the case, it should be returned in a similar fashion the
ensuing day. If, however, a call is really made, that is,
if the lady comes in, two days may be allowed to elapse
before returning it. In ordinary visiting a call should
be returned within about three weeks, cards within a
fortnight. One call in a season, or one in the before-Easter,
and the other in the after-Easter season, is the average for
acquaintances.*

*Morning calls (so designated because they are paid
before dinner) are made between the hours of four
and seven ... Twenty minutes is the usual extent of an
afternoon call.*

As to the appearance of a visiting card, *How to Entertain;
or Etiquette for Visitors* (1876) has the following advice.

*A lady's card may be either glazed or plain. Some people
omit the prefix 'Miss' to their names on a card. This is an
affectation of simplicity which takes away all appearance
of that quality.*
   *It is a thing unknown in English society, though the
fashion on the continent, for a lady to have only her
Christian name and her surname on her card.*

How to treat a snake bite

In many countries around the world snakes can prove to
be a menace, slithering into houses, depositing themselves
in quiet corners and waiting for the unsuspecting
householder to step unawares into their orbit. Today
medics are generally furnished with antidotes to snake
venom and thus the threat from a snake bite is lessened.
However, back in the day, treatment for snake bites
was somewhat more improvised, as Edmund C. P. Hull
describes in *The European in India* (1874).

*Although no antidote has yet been discovered for snake
poison, yet some measures may be tried to save the life of*

the persons under its influence. First apply a tight bandage
or ligature a few inches above the wound; cut out the
bitten part mercilessly, or freely scarify it with a lancet or
penknife by incisions all round. There need be no fear of
the bleeding if the part cut out is on the fingers or toes; but
if it continue too profuse, steady firm pressure with the
thumb will arrest it. A red-hot iron, or nitric or carbolic
acid may now be pressed into the bitten part, or applied at
first if the patient will not submit to excision or incision.
Sucking the wound should also be tried, but care must
be taken that the party performing this operation has no
broken surface on his mouth or lips.

Twenty drops of the strongest liquor ammoniae, or eau
de luce, diluted with water; or half a glass of brandy or
rum, should be given at once, and repeated every fifteen
minutes till reaction sets in. Mustard poultices, or a cloth
soaked in liquid ammoniae, should be applied over the
stomach and heart; and the patient should be encouraged to
walk about a little in order to combat the drowsiness which
so commonly comes on.

How to read moles

Nine Pennyworth of Wit for a Penny (1750) informed
their readers how to read their fortune by examining the
positioning of their moles.

Moles in the face particularly, and those in other parts of
the body are very significant as to good or bad fortune.
A mole on the left side of the forehead, denotes the

party will get rich by tillage, building and planting.

A mole on the right side of the forehead, promises happy contentment of life, a loving state in matrimony, &c.

A mole on the middle of the forehead, denotes a person subject to sickness, and other afflictions.

A mole on the left side of the temple, promises loss and affliction to either sex in the first part of their age; but happiness by overcoming them in the end.

A mole on the eyebrow signifies speedy marriage and a good husband.

A mole on the left cheek, inclining towards the lower part of the ear, denotes loss in goods, and crosses by children; threatens a woman with death in child-bed.

A mole on the nose, foretells the birth of many children, and persons powerful in generation.

A mole on the right corner of the mouth, near the jaw, promises happy days to either sex; but on the left side, unlawful copulation, and much loss thereby.

A mole on the left shoulder denotes labour, travel and sorrow.

How to set a sundial

Cassell's Home Encyclopedia (1934) contains this rather excellent, if not demanding, advice on how to set a sundial.

The dial is attached to the top of the pillar by screwing it down with four screws to the wooden blocks embedded in the concrete capping. The gnomon should point north and south, with the highest pointing towards the north.

A sundial made for one particular place is quite useless for another place in a different latitude. Before setting a sundial it is essential to know whether the sun is fast or slow of the clock. Sundials show apparent time whilst clocks measure equal or mean time so that if a perfectly regulated clock were set to apparent solar time it would agree with the sundial only on four days of the year. A solar day is the period which elapses between two successive returns of the sun to the meridian. The moment the sun reaches

its highest point in the heavens, that is, the highest point above the horizon, it is true noon. Sometimes the sun is as much as 14 min 28 sec after the clock, and at others 16 min 18 sec before the clock at XII o'clock noon. Mean time is that shown by clocks generally, the day of 24 hours being obtained by taking the average of the solar days of the year. Place the dial upon the platform and move it about until the shadow cast by the gnomon on the dial shows the correct time within a few minutes.

To read the time by sundial, stand on its north side. The forenoon or morning hours will then be on the right-hand side of the dial whilst the afternoon hours will be on the left. At noon the shadow of the gnomon will fall within the space between the two lines at XII o'clock.

When the dial is in the correct position, mark the platform or capstone through the holes in the dial for fixing the screws. Finally adjust and fix the dial at XII o'clock noon. Of course it can be fixed at other times but XII is the best. The sundial and clock coincide only four times in a year, about April 15, June 14, Aug 31 and Dec 25 and it will be found convenient to fix the dial on or near one of these days, provided the sun is shining.

How to refuse a proposal of marriage

The Etiquette of Courtship and Matrimony (1865) recommends exercising the utmost delicacy when rebuffing a suitor.

When a lady rejects the proposal of a gentleman, her behaviour should be characterised by the most delicate feeling towards one who, in offering her his hand, has proved his desire to confer upon her, by this implied preference for her above all other women, the greatest honour it is in his power to offer. Therefore, if she have no love for him, she ought at least to evince a tender regard for his feelings.

No woman of proper feeling would regard her rejection of an offer of marriage from a worthy man as a matter of triumph: her feeling on such an occasion should be one of regretful sympathy with him for the pain she is unavoidably compelled to inflict. Nor should such a rejection be unaccompanied with some degree of self-examination on her part, to discern whether any lightness of demeanour or tendency to flirtation may have given

rise to a false hope of her favouring his suit. At all events,
no lady should ever treat a man who has so honoured her
with the slightest disrespect or frivolous disregards, nor
ever unfeelingly parade a more favoured suitor before one
whom she has refused.

How to train a falcon

The sport of falconry originated in the Far East and
from the time of King Alfred it became a popular sport
amongst the aristocracy in Britain. To hawk partridge,
magpies or rooks requires very large expanses of open
country. Due to the enclosure of the land with hedgerows
and suchlike, and the increasing popularity of shooting
game, falconry became harder to practise, as suitable
locations became few and far between. This combined
with the amount of time and effort required to train up
a falcon meant that falconry became a lost skill, glimpses
of which can be afforded by wild bird displays put on at
county fairs and raptor centres.

Practical Falconry by Gage Earle Freeman (1869) gives
advice on which bird to choose, and where to find the
beast once selected.

Let us suppose that he has no game – no rabbits even – but
that there is an open common near him affording rooks,
magpies, pigeons, larks. Not the goshawk then; his hawks
are the peregrine and merlin. Does he live near moors on
which he can hawk? Still the peregrine. On fairly-open
partridge ground? The peregrine still. But the goshawk is

*the bird for a very enclosed country; and, should he care to
fly the sparrowhawk, he may add that.*

    *This is just a rough and general answer to the question,
'what sort of hawks a man ought to have?' And now we
come to the second point 'How is he to procure them?'*

    *As to the peregrine, I can only say generally that the
species breed on high and dangerous rocks, both by the sea
and inland; and that young birds are obtained by falconers,
very frequently from Scotland … It is a difficult matter to
procure goshawks, but they may occasionally be got from
one of the professional falconers, or from the Regent's
Park Gardens. As a rule they are imported either from
France or from Germany.*

    *Merlins are often found on the moors. They build on the
ground, but are not often offered for sale … Sparrowhawks
are easily procured. The gamekeeper of a wooded manor
is almost sure to be able to help the falconer. Hobbies
are so rare that it is hardly worthwhile to mention them;
but if procured they should be treated like merlins. The
jer-falcons can be obtained from Iceland, Greenland, or
Norway, by sending over a falconer to catch them.*

James Edmund Harting in his *Hints on the Management
of Hawks* (1898) offers up the following advice on choosing
a falcon.

*When choosing a hawk, see that the eyes are full and
bright: sunken eyes and contracted pupils are a sure
indication of ill-health. The tongue and inside of the
mouth should be pink: a furred tongue of a whitey-brown
colour is a bad sign. The head should be flat, the shoulders*

*broad, the wings long and well crossed over the tail
when closed. The pectoral muscles (under the wing)
should be full and firm to the touch, not soft and flabby.
The flight feathers should be perfect (ten in each wing),
and should have good broad webs. It is easy to examine
them after hooding the bird by gently expanding each wing
in turn. The thighs should be muscular, the feet large and
strong. They may be tested by carrying the hawk hooded
against the wind, when you will soon discover if the bird
in holding on has a good grip.*

To begin training the hawk, a falconer must do the
following.

*A newly-caught hawk should be kept on the perch for some
time, hooded and unhooded, fed regularly on the hand,
and carried about for a few days before it is put out on the
block. If put out too soon, the tameness which it has begun
to acquire is lost, and it flies wildly off the block to the end
of its tether, striving vainly to make its escape, and paying
no regard to lure or meat.*

*It will be found that the bird when hungry, will readily
jump from the perch, or block, to the hand, or on the lure,
if the latter be thrown on the ground. All that is then
necessary is to remove the leash and tie a long light line to
the swivel (which remains attached to the jesses during the
training, but never when the trained hawk is flown), and
holding this line (a plaited fishing line is best) in the left
hand when the hawk is called off to the lure, the length of
flight may be increased daily, until finally the line may
be dispensed with altogether. It is important to bear in*

mind that the hawk should never be flown except when it is
hungry and when it is therefore more likely to be obedient
to the lure. Before discard the line or 'creance', as it is
technically termed, a live bird, of the kind to be afterwards
flown at, should be given in a shorter creance, and the
hawk allowed not only to kill it, but to make a good meal
off it.

The hawk is now ready to be flown for the first time.

When flying a hawk loose for the first time, it is most
important to guard against disappointment, and care
should be taken to secure such a flight that the hawk will be
almost certain to kill. The method I pursue with a Merlin
is to carry it hooded over likely ground for a Lark, until
I put one up. As soon as it has pitched again and I have
marked it down, I take off the hood and walk straight up
wind to the spot. The Lark again rises, the hawk is off the
hand in a second, and, if previously well exercised to
the lure, is almost sure to kill. I then allow her to plume
the quarry and have a few mouthfuls before I take her up,
letting her finish the meal on my glove.

What the falconer has to aim at in the field is to make
his hawk understand that he does not approach her to take
away the food from her, but to help her to secure and enjoy
it. As soon as that feeling is established between bird and
man, all will go well. The hawk will improve daily, and
the falconer's pleasure will be proportionally increased.

Harting goes on to describe his experience when taking a
goshawk hunting for the first time.

It was an anxious moment as we walked the next afternoon about a rough bramble-covered common, in anticipation of getting a good flight at a rabbit. A couple of beaters tried the most likely looking bushes, while we stood in the open, 'with grey Goshawk on hand' (as Chaucer hath it), waiting for a rabbit to bolt.

At length we were rewarded. Out flashed a bunny, and across the open like lightning. Unfortunately, the space to be crossed was too short; and, although the hawk left the hand instantly, the rabbit just contrived to reach a bush before she could seize him; but so plucky was she that she went in after him, and got so far into the bush – through which, of course, he made his escape – that we had to use our knives and cut her out to prevent damage to feathers. This was bad luck for a beginning, but the hawk was keen, and we could easily find another for her. This we did, and she took him in style – a great big buck rabbit, who thought to get rid of her by jumping into the air and kicking like any 'buckjumper', but she stuck to him well till we killed him, when she was duly rewarded.

How to understand the language of falconry

The following is an extracted glossary of terms used in hawking, as taken from *The Badminton Library of Sports and Pastimes: Coursing and Falconry* by Harding Cox and the Honourable Gerald Lascelles (1892).

Bind: To seize and hold quarry in the air.
Cadge: A frame of wood with padded edges upon which

hawks sit when carried to the field.
Cast: A couple of hawks.
Castings: Fur or feathers given to hawk, together with its
food, to promote digestion.
Enter: To train a hawk to a particular quarry.
Eyess, or Eyas: A hawk taken from the nest.
Hack: A state of liberty in which young eyesses are kept
for some weeks to enable them to gain power of wing.
Haggard: A hawk captured after she has assumed the
mature plumage i.e. two years old at least.
Hood: A cap of leather use for blinding a hawk, so as to
bring her under proper control.
Imp: To repair broken feathers.
Jesses: Leather straps about six inches long permanently
secured to the legs of a hawk.
Leash: A leathern thong fastened by a swivel to the jesses
in order to secure the hawk to a perch or block.
Mews: The place where hawks are kept.
Passage: The regular flight of any quarry to or from its
feeding ground.
Point, to make: The perpendicular shoot up of a hawk over
the exact spot where quarry has put in.
Put in: The quarry is 'put in' when driven to take refuge in
some covert.
Serving a hawk: Driving out the quarry which has 'put in'
to the hawk as she waits overhead.
Tiercel, tercel or tassel: The male hawks as opposed to the
female; he being a 'tierce' or third smaller in size.

How to make lip balm

The following recipe for homemade lip balm (although modern readers may have trouble sourcing some of the ingredients) can be found in *A Shilling's Worth of Practical Receipts* (1856).

Put a quarter of an ounce of Benjamin*, storax**, and spermaceti***, two-penny worth of alkanet root, a juicy apple chopped, a bunch of black grapes bruised, a quarter of a pound of unsalted butter, and two ounces of bees' wax into a new tin saucepan. Simmer gently till all is dissolved, and then strain it through linen. When cold, melt it again, and pour it into small pots or boxes; if to make cakes, use the bottom of tea cups.

*Also known as Benzoin, this is the resin from an evergreen tree (*Styrax benzoin*) used as an astringent or antiseptic.
** Storax (or Styrax) is a balsam taken from the bark of the *Liquidambar orientalis* tree, generally used as a perfume or expectorant.
*** Spermaceti is a wax found in the head of a sperm or bottlenose whale. It was commonly used in cosmetics and as an industrial lubricant.

How to address a Maharajah

Hob-nobbing with the local gentry was one of the chief delights of the English in India. However, the vagaries of greeting the many and varied high-born Indians was something of a mystery to those brought up with only the anglocentric *Debrett's* to guide them through such a minefield. Thus most Anglo-Indians referred to tomes such as the excellent *Hints on Indian Etiquette Specially Designed for the Use of Europeans* by Iftikhar Husain (1911), who advised that the following form should be followed when writing a letter to a Maharajah or similar-titled person of higher rank than you.

You of exalted rank, lofty position and of noble birth, may you have increased graciousness.

And he advises that one might sign off with the following.

Your obedient servant
or
The lowest of the low
or
Humble as dust

The Anglo-Hindoostanee Hand-book; or, Stranger's Self-interpreter and Guide to Colloquial and General Intercourse with the Natives of India (1850) describes an altogether more complicated system of salutations and greetings that should be employed.

The natives of Bengal and Hindoostan observe numerous forms of salutations according to the respective ranks of the parties between whom they are observed; superiors, as in Europe, receiving various ceremonious forms of respect from their inferiors whose salutes in many instances, and particularly in the courts of native princes, are merely acknowledged by an inclination of the head, or a movement of the right hand.

The handbook then describes the six most frequently used salutations.

The salutations of inferiors to superiors are usually expressed more by actions than words ...

1. Sulám – literally Salutation; Peace; Safety ... In Calcutta and other Indian mercantile towns where there is frequent intercourse in the transaction of business between very mixed classes of people – Native and European, the Sulam, expressed by the simple action of touching the forehead with the right hand, commonly forms the sole ceremony of salutation both at meeting and parting; though the action is usually and properly accompanied with the utterance of the word itself, and hence the common verbal salutation of natives to Europeans – Sahib Sulam! Literally – Sir Salutation!

2. Bun'dug'ee: literally Slavery: Service: Devotion: Worship: Compliment. The action of the Bundugee differs from the sulam simply in the additional form of 'meeting the motion of the hand with a gentle inclination of the head forwards'. As a salutation the Bundugee is most commonly observed by the upper ranks of Natives and Europeans to their equals and superiors.

3. Kornish: literally Salutation: Adoration. As a salutation the Kornish differs from the action of the Bundugee in the further form of bending the body as well as the head.

4. Tus'leem : literally Delivery; Consignment; Health: Security: recommending to the care and protection of another; saluting most respectfully. The action of the Tusleem 'consists in touching the ground with the fingers, and then making Sulam' which form is sometimes thrice repeated.

5. Kud'um'bo'see: literally Kissing the feet: Obeisance:
Respects: As a salutation the kud'um'bo'see is performed as
a token of humiliation or reverence before parents or great
people only, and is expressed by kissing the foot or touching
it with the right hand, or touching or kissing the edge of
the carpet or mat on which the party so honoured may be
sitting.
6. Usht'ang – Adoration performed with eight members, i.e.
the hands, feet, thighs, breasts, eyes, head, speech and mind.
An exclusively hindoo salutation performed in token or
adoration or reverence by hindoos before their idols, priests
or superiors; the action 'consists prostrating themselves on
the ground, with the arms stretched out and the palms of
the hands joined together.'

The handbook goes on to offer some counsel on the
etiquette of visiting.

Natives of high rank – hindoo or moohummudun, when
receiving visits of ceremony usually retain their seats,
unless the visitors be their equals, or otherwise European
officials of high rank in the service of the British
government, in which event the parties visited rise and
advance a certain distance according to the degree of
ceremonious respect that the rank of the visitor may claim
or circumstances suggest.

Having successfully greeted your host, the visitor must
then remember to leave in the appropriate style, making
sure they take careful note of the elaborate hints that
indicate that they have over-stayed their welcome:

Immediately ere parting the parties visited usually present to each of their guests Utr-pan (a cud of betel-pepper leaves), and then, with bottles, sprinkle rose-water over their handkerchiefs or clothes, which ceremony if performed ere the visitors themselves be prepared to go, is the usual polite intimation that their departure is desired.

How to predict the weather from nature

Britons have always had an obsession with the weather, living as they do on an island at the mercy of the ever-changing elements. As a result many people used signs from nature (rather than just looking out of the window) to try and predict the weather. In the comprehensive work *A Companion to the Weather Glass* (1796) the author includes an extract from *Shepherd of Banbury's Rules: To Judge the Changes of the Weather* (1748), which reveals the following tips for anticipating the climate.

SUN
If the sun rise red and fiery – wind and rain.
If cloudy, and it soon decrease – certain fair weather.

MOON
Horns of the moon obscure – rain.
When the moon is red – wind.
On the fourth day of the new moon, if bright, with sharp horns – no winds nor rain till the month be finished.

STARS

When stars shoot precipitant through the sky —
approaching wind.

CLOUDS

Clouds small and round, like a dapple-grey with a north
wind — fair weather for two or three days.
Large, like rocks — great showers.
If small clouds increase — much rain.
If large clouds decrease — fair weather.
Clouds in summer or harvest, when the wind has been
south two or three days, and it grows very hot, and you see
clouds rise with great white tops like towers, as if one were
upon the top of another, and joined together with black on
the nether side — there will be thunder and rain suddenly.
If two such clouds arise, one on either hand — it is time to
make haste to shelter.
If you see a cloud rise against the wind or side-wind, when
that cloud comes up to you, the wind will blow the same
way that the clouds came. And the same rule holds of a
clear place, when all the sky is equally thick, except one
clear edge.

MISTS

If mists rise in low ground and soon vanish — fair weather.
If they rise to the hill tops — rain in a day or two.
A general mist before the sun rises near the full moon —
fair weather.
If in the new moon — rain in the old.
If in the old moon — rain in the new.

Not only could The Shepherd predict the weather by observing the sky, but he also recommended the following ways of reading the weather through the observation of animals, noting that winds are forecast by:

Cormorants swiftly returning from sea to land, making a great noise.
The heron forsaking the fens and soaring aloft.

Whereas rain is forecast by:

Cranes forsaking the valleys.
Heifers snuffling the air.
Swallows fluttering about the lakes.
Frogs croaking.
Ants conveying their eggs from their cells.
Ravens flocking together, making a great noise.
Bees in clusters humming about the hive.

Furnished with this insight, please do ensure that the next time you see a heifer snuffling the air, ravens flocking noisily or a crane forsaking the valley, you should remember to get your washing in.

How to make mushroom ketchup

A common condiment in Victorian times, *A Shilling's Worth of Practical Receipts* (1856) offers this recipe for mushroom ketchup.

Gather the broad flapped and red gilded mushrooms
before the sun has discoloured them; wipe, and break them
into an earthen pan. To every three handfuls throw in one
handful of salt, stir them two or three times a day till the
salt is dissolved, and the mushrooms are liquid. Bruise
what bits remain, set the whole over a gentle fire till the
goodness is extracted; strain the hot liquor through a fine
hair sieve, boil it gently with allspice, whole black pepper,
ginger, horse-radish, and an onion or some shallots, with
two or three laurel leaves. Some use garlic, all the different
spices, mustard seeds &c. but if not wanted for long
keeping it is preferable without anything but salt. After
simmering some time, and well skimming, strain it into
bottles; when cold close them with a cork and bladder. If
again boiled at the end of three months with fresh spice
and a stick of sliced horse radish, it will keep very well for
at least a year; but it seldom does this, unless it be boiled a
second time.

How to pan for gold

The gold rush in California began in 1848 when a
carpenter from New Jersey, James Wilson Marshall, found
some gold at Coloma, California. Reports soon spread that
gold nuggets were so prevalent they could be plucked,
whole, from the surface of the ground – further swelling
the numbers making the journey. The rush peaked
in 1852 and continued through to 1855, as more than
300,000 people flocked to the area to make their fortune,
transforming California in the process.

Gold Dust: How to Find it and How to Mine it (1898) describes how to identify a potential gold mine.

It remains a fact, that you are more likely to find it among some kinds of rocks than others, and it may be set down as a rule that, when all the rocks you can find in a certain region lie in horizontal layers, whether they are of slate, limestone, sandstone or lava, and the boulders in streams consists of the same material, it is not worth while to look for gold in that region.

The largest and best mines are usually round near where the longest and strongest traces of eruptive rock cross that part of the country rock which carries the gold. And, sometimes it is the eruptive itself which furnishes all the gold, though its step-mother, the quartz, gets the honor.

The river is another promising location in which to find gold.

If you are seeking gold, the easiest place to find the trace is among the boulders at the water's edge at low water, and at the head of the rapids.

Find a place on the low bars, where the current is strong enough to carry away all the lightest gravel when the water is up, but not strong enough to tear out the boulders as large as your head. If you find a few points of rough bedrock sticking up, it is the best in sight. Now, with a pick or bar, turn out a few boulders and take the sand and fine gravel from among them and pan it carefully. If you get a large handful of black sand, and not a color of gold, try two more such bars, and if they yield the same, go down the stream, for there is but a very slim chance of any pay on any branch above.

When you have found a creek that prospects better, or yields coarser gold than the river does above the mouth of it, follow it up. Take notice as to what kind of rock the gravel is made up of, and the nature of the bedrock, and when you pass a rapid or find the channel widening out, so as to form a bar on either side of the stream, try for bedrock, the same as on a river, at both ends of the bar, and don't forget the small gulches.

The best claims on a river or large creek are most likely to be where the channel is of moderate width, and the bedrock has a natural grade of seven to eighteen inches to the rod. Deep holes in a channel very rarely pay for cleaning out.

Once a good position has been found, the prospector must next start to pan.

The most important tool for a beginner is a gold pan, which should be made in one piece, of Russia iron or sheet steel, pressed into shape and stiffened with a steel wire in the rim. A pressed frying pan with the handle cut off is a good substitute, if there is no grease in it.

Having found dirt likely to contain gold, and water with which to test it, take about ten pounds of dirt into the pan and put it under the water; then stir it and shake it until the mud is softened, and the gravel and sand is loose and clean, washing away the thin mud as fast as you make it. Next hold the pan half out of the water at a low angle, and shake, roll and dip it in such a manner that the heavy parts will sink and the light parts be washed over the side. When you have washed it all out but the last handful, or when you begin to see a streak of black sand along the edge of the gravel, you should take care not to wash the gold over the side, which can be prevented by holding the pan flat and shaking it occasionally. When you have washed out all of the white sand and taken out the pebbles, examine the black sand carefully by rolling it around in the pan of water; and if any portion is much heavier than the rest, examine that by crushing it in your teeth, or otherwise; if it is malleable it is metal, and unless it is a piece of a bullet, may be gold.

In an 1852 book, *The Chemistry of Gold*, the author further describes the methods a prospector might use to try and extract some gold.

The most primitive gold-washing apparatus is a wooden or metallic dish, varying in size as well as in shape and material in different localities ... The general principles on which the employment of these instruments depends, has been already indicated, but to use them well requires great practice and experience. In either case the object is to isolate the gold; this isolation being effected by various manipulative jerks and gyrations, and requiring much dexterity.

A great improvement on pans, of whatever shape, is the cradle, as it is termed; an instrument which derives its name from a resemblance in shape and action to its prototype. The gold-washer's cradle consists of a trough-like body elevated on rockers, not horizontally but at an

angle, and supplied with a sieve-like head, for the purpose
of intercepting large masses of ore and stone. The body
is covered transversely by wooden bars a few inches high,
and capable of removal. The cradle is worked as follows:
one man throws in a portion of material to be washed upon
the sieve-like top, meanwhile another individual imparts a
rocking motion, and water is poured on. The result will be
anticipated. All the lighter particles are caused to rise by
the rocking motion, to be suspended in the flowing water
and to pass over the bars, whilst the gold is left behind and
can be easily removed.

In 1851, a rival gold rush began in Australia after gold was discovered in Victoria. *The Gold Fields of Australia* was published in 1852, and does not try to disguise the rivalry between the two gold-mining countries.

Sometimes the gold particles are so small, and so mixed
with black sand, that it takes great pains to separate the
metal. This is mostly the case with Californian gold. Thus
mixed up with sand, the deposit is drawn off, dried in the
sun, and the sand is afterwards separated by blowing off
the sand, or, what is the more usual process in California,
by the process of amalgamation with quicksilver. This
unties with the particles of gold, rejecting the sand; and
then, by the application of a moderate heat, the quicksilver
is evaporated, leaving the pure gold behind and the former
metal, being distilled into a receiver, is collected for use
over again. But this process is too slow for the Australians.
The gold is found in particles so large, as to render it a
waste of time for them to separate it by quicksilver …

The above fact, however, we think, sufficiently proves the much greater richness of the gold mines of Australia, when compared to those of California. Indeed, the Californians are already emigrating to Australia in considerable numbers, attracted by the far greater richness of the soil.

Identifying true gold was one of the problems faced by the prospectors. As a result *Gold Dust: How to Find it and How to Mine it* (1898) offers the following advice on how to test for gold.

To test it, melt it into a button, hammer it out flat and boil it in nitric acid and water for several minutes. If it comes out black there was silver in it, but heating it red-hot will make it yellow and nearly pure. Gold, and nothing else, will stand this test.

Several things are often mistaken for gold by the uninitiated. Among them are chalcopyrite, or copper pyrite, which is easily crushed to a dark green powder; iron pyrite, very hard, yields black powder; yellow mica, very light weight, splits in thin scales; streaks of brass from boot nails, always on the outside of the rock; shreds of copper and brass, from giant caps or elsewhere; and also yellow silicate of lead, called packer's gold, which is the same weight and color as fine shot, and only determined by melting with borax or crushing to powder, which makes the water yellow.

Having discovered a vein of gold to mine, the prospector must set up camp. *Gold Dust: How to Find it and How to Mine it* (1898) recommends building a wikiup, thus:

*By building a wikiup in a dry place, just big enough to
roll under, leaving one side open and making a log fire
alongside, a very light bed is made sufficient in ordinary
weather. To build the wikiup, set up two forked sticks about
two feet high and seven feet apart and lay a pole therein;
gather bark or sticks and moss to roof it over, about three
feet wide, using a six-inch log for the back. Put in a few
inches of dry grass or leaves and spread your bedding on
that. By using a little care a bark roof can be made to keep
out the rain, and it reflects the heat from the fire quite well.
Make a fire opposite the middle, and the lodging is ready.*

With camp ready, the tired prospector must next eat.

*To bake prospectors bread, put a pint of flour in the gold
pan, add a pinch of salt, a teaspoonful of baking powder,
a spoonful of sugar, and mix it well together, then add a
cup of cold water, mix and knead into stiff dough. Grease
the frying pan and get it hot, then press half of the dough
into the bottom of the pan, making it a little thinner in the
centre than around the sides; set the pan on some hot coals
until a thin crust forms on the bottom, so that it will slip in
the pan; now set it at an angle facing the fire, putting any
old thing under the handle to hold it up, having a fire that
will turn it brown in ten or fifteen minutes, tossing it as
needed.*

The gold rush made a few people very rich (in California
alone more than two billion dollars' worth of gold was
found from 1848 to 1855) but most eked out a meagre
existence, scratching a living from the traces of gold they

extracted from the ground. Large industrialised mining companies soon dominated the gold fields of California, spelling an end to the era of the plucky prospector armed with just a pick and a gold pan.

How to dry-clean clothes

With the convenience of the washing machine and the proximity of the local dry-cleaner we have lost the art of caring for our own clothes. However, *The Family Dyer and Scourer* by William Tucker (1817) reveals how to dry-clean your clothes on your kitchen table.

First examining where the spots of grease are, dip your brush in warm gall and strike over the greasy places, when the grease will immediately disappear, rinse it off in cold water; dry by the fire, then take sand, such as is bought at the oil shops, and laying your coat flat on a table, strew this sand over it, and knocking your brush on it, beat the sand into the cloth, the sand should be a little damp. Then brush it out with a hard brush, and it will bring all the filth out with it ... In the summer time when the dust gets into clothes, &c. after they have been well shook and brushed again, pour a drop or two of the oil of olives into the palm of your hand, rub this over your soft brush, strike your coat with it, and this will brighten the colour if either blue, black or green.

How to bait a hook

*What can be more delightful than angling? Not indeed
so much on account of the fish we may catch, but for the
pleasantness of the recreation itself, for the cool streams,
the shady trees, the little sunny nooks, the tiny or gigantic
cascades, the meandering rills, the still pools, 'with sedges
overhung;' the picturesque mill-wheels, the deep mill-
ponds, 'smooth sheeted by the flood;' and above all, for the
hair-breadth escapes, for the duckings, for the huzzards, for
the triumphs.*

The *Handbook of Fishing* (1867) paints this delightful
picture of angling. The book goes on to describe the
methods for baiting a hook.

*To bait a hook with a worm, use the following method:
First enter the point of the hook close to the top of the
worm's head, and carry it carefully down to within a
quarter of an inch of its tail; to do which you must gently
squeeze or work up the worm with your left thumb and
finger, while with your right you are gradually working
the hook downwards. The small lively piece of the worm
at the point of the hook moving about will entice the fish;
but mind, if too much of the worm hangs loose, though
it may entice fish to nibble, yet they will seldom take the
whole in their mouth, so as to enable the angler to hook
them ... Therefore to bait a hook well with a worm is
necessary to insure hitting a fish when you strike; and it
consists in drawing the worm without injuring it (use him
as you would a friend ...) quite over and up the shank of*

the hook, leaving only a small lively part of the tail below.

The following are the principle baits and where to find them.

1. Lob-worms are found in gardens or churchyards, late in the evening; they have a red head, a streak down the back, and a broad tail. This is a good worm for salmon, chub, trout, barbell, eels and large perch.

2. Brandling is found in old dunghills, rotten earth or cowdung, and the best in tanners' bark. It is a good bait for any kind of fish.

3. The Marsh-worm is found in marshy ground, or on the banks of rivers; and is a good bait for trout, perch, gudgeon, grayling and bream.

4. The Tagtail is found in marly lands or meadows after a shower; and is a good bait for trout when the water is muddy.

5. The Ash-grub is found in the bark of trees. It is a good bait for grayling, dace, roach or chub.

6. Cowdung-bait is found under cowdung, from May to Michaelmas; and is good bait for grayling, dace, roach or chub.

7. Caterpillars can be found on almost every tree or plant. Almost any small caterpillar will answer.

8. The cabbage-caterpillar is found on cabbages.

9. The crabtree-worm can be taken by beating the branches of the crab apple.

10. Gentils. These are bred in putrid liver, or may be obtained from the butchers. They are an excellent bait for all kinds of fish.

11. Cad is found in the ditches, or on the sides of stony brooks. It is an excellent bait for all kinds of fish.

12. Flag-worms are found among flags in old pits or ponds, and are good bait for grayling, tench, bream, carp, roach, and dace.

13. Grasshoppers, found in sun-burnt grass, are good bait for various kinds of fish.

14. Wasp-grubs are to be obtained from wasps' nests, and are a good bait for most fish that will take gentils (wasp-grubs will keep better and be easier to fit on the hook, if they are baked for half an hour).

15. Beetles are found everywhere, and sometimes in cowdung. They are a capital bait for chub.

16. Salmon-spawn is a good bait for trout, chub, and other fish; but must be prepared in a peculiar way before it can be used.

17. White-bread paste is prepared by dipping white bread in honey, and working it in the palm of the hand. It is a good bait for carp, tench, chub, or roach.

18. Cheese paste is made with rotten cheese and bread, worked up in the hand. It is a good bait for chub.

19. Wheat paste is made by bruising wheat and working it with milk, and makes a good ground bait.

20. Ground bait should be used in the spot about to be fished, and, if possible, the night before, and should be fresh. For carp, chub, roach or dace, use white bread soaked in water, and mixed with bran and pollard. For roach, dace, and bleak, mix clay and bran together in balls the size of a pigeon's egg. For barbell, chandler's greaves, boiled and worked up into a ball with clay. For carp, tench, and eels, malt soaked in water is good; or gentils may be thrown in.

How to make British anchovies

The strong, flavoursome anchovy have long been a popular fish, however genuine Mediterranean anchovies could be expensive and hard to source, so *The Art and Mystery of Curing, Preserving, and Potting all Kinds of Meats, Game, and Fish* (1864) contains this recipe to create an English version of the delicacy.

If it were worthwhile to favour the deception, you must select your fish from out of half a bushel of the freshest you can get, retaining only the middle-sized ones, for real Gorgana fish are never so large as our large sprats, and never so small as our little ones, and yours should also be all of the same size. Pull off the heads – not cutting them – in a rough manner, and draw out the gut. Wash not and wipe not the fish, but put them in straight-sided unglazed earthen jars, wood is preferable, in layers alternately with this mixture:

Bay salt	*2 lb.*
*Sal prunelle**	*2 oz.*
Cochineal, in fine powder	*2 oz.*

Pressing them down as you proceed, and letting the top layer of the mixture be at least two inches thick. Get cork bungs cut to fit well, and secure them with plenty of melted resin. Bury the jars in dry sand in your cellar or store room, 'out of the way', and do not disturb them for nine months, or till the next sprat season. A fortnight before you would broach your 'prize', dissolve

*Gum dragon***	*2 oz.*
Sal prunelle	*2 oz.*
*Red sanders****	*1 oz.*

in a pint of boiled water, and strain it through flannel,
pour it evenly over the contents of your jars or vessels;
secure the bung again, and in a week or less, turn the
receptacles upside-down for a day or two, and then again
set them upright. This is called 'feeding' them. And when
all is done, without the aid of 'brick-dust', or what is as
bad, 'Armenian Bole', to give them a fine red colour, the
said 'British anchovies' may do to make anchovy sauce of,
with other ingredients, but to bring to table, with dry or
buttered toast, as Gorgana fish – Oh never!

* Sal prunelle is nitrate of potash cast into round moulds.
** Gum dragon is tragacanth, the sap of a Middle Eastern plant.
*** Red sanders is red sandalwood, from a small tree native to India.
In this context the sawdust of the tree would probably have been used
to give the fish a red hue.

How to make a love charm

The Book of Charms and Ceremonies: whereby all may
have the opportunity of obtaining any object they desire by
'Merlin' (1892) offers the following instructions on how to
make a love charm.

Agrippa says that the hair off the belly of a goat, tied
into knots and concealed in the roof of the house of the
beloved, will produce furious love, whereby the maiden
will not be able to withstand the entreaties of her lover,
but will be so enchanted with him that marriage will soon
take place.

How to tell the age of a horse from its teeth (in rhyme)

When attempting any sort of complex investigation of a horse's many sharp teeth in order to ascertain its age, what you really want are simple, clear instructions. What you don't want is for those instructions to be bland and boring. Luckily, *Horse Sense: Jumping, driving, shoeing, bits, foods, breaking* (1911) has provided a delightful poem for the very purpose.

To tell the age of any horse,
Inspect the lower jaw, of course.
The six front teeth the tale will tell,
And every doubt and fear dispel.

Two middle 'nippers' you behold
Before the colt is two weeks old.
Before eight weeks two more will come;
Eight months, the 'corners' cut the gum.

Two outside grooves will disappear
From middle two in just one year.
In two years from the second pair;
In three, the corners, too, are bare.

At two, the middle 'nippers' drop;
At three, the second pair can't stop.
When four years old, the third pair goes;
At five, a full new set he shows.

The deep black spots will pass from view
At six years from the middle two.
The second pair at seven years;
At eight the spot each 'corner' clears.

From middle 'nippers' upper jaw,
At nine the black spots will withdraw.
The second pair at ten are white;
Eleven finds the 'corners' light.

As time goes on, the horsemen know,
The oval teeth three-sided grow;
They longer get, project before,
Till twenty, when we know no more.

How to dye fabrics with dyes from British plants

Ethel M. Mairet, in her 1924 book *Vegetable Dyes: being a book of recipes and other information useful to the dyer*, explains how once-common native vegetable dyes have now become scarce.

On the introduction of foreign dye woods and other dyes during the 17th and 18th centuries, the native dye plants were rapidly displaced, except in some out of the way places such as the Highlands and parts of Ireland.

The majority of these plants are not very important as dyes, and could not probably now be collected in sufficient quantities. Some few, however, are important, such as woad,

weld, heather, walnut, alder, oak, some lichens.
The yellow dyes are the most plentiful and many of these
are good fast colours. Practically no good red, in quantity,
is obtainable. Madder is the only reliable red dye among
plants, and that is no longer indigenous in England.

Mairet goes on to list some of the native plants that can be
used to dye cloth red ...

Birch Betula alba — *Fresh inner bark*
Common Sorrel Rumex acetosa — *Roots*
Dyer's woodruff Asperula tinctoria — *Roots*
Marsh potential Potentilla comarum — *Roots*

And plants which dye blue ...

Elder Sambucus nigra — *Berries*
Privet Ligustrum vulgare — *Berries with alum and salt.*
Yellow iris Iris pseudacorus — *Roots*
Sloe Prunus communis — *Fruit (on boiling sloes, their*
juice becomes red, and the red dye which it imparts to
linen changes, when washed with soap, into a bluish colour,
which is permanent.)

And those plants which dye yellow ...

Ash Fraximinus excelsior — *Fresh inner bark*
Barberry Berberis vulgaris — *Stem and root*
Common dock Rumex obtusifolius — *Root*
Crab apple Pyrus malus — *Fresh inner bark*

Plants which dye green …

Elder Sambucus nigra — *Leaves with alum*
Lily of the valley Convalaria majalis — *Leaves*

Some plants which dye brown …

Birch Betula alba — *bark*
Onion — *skins*
Walnuts — *root and green husks of nut*

Those plants which dye purple …

Bryony Bryonia dioica — *Berries*
Dandelion Taraxacum dens-leonis — *Roots*
Elder Sambucus nigra — *Berries with alum, a violet; with alum and salt, a lilac colour.*

And finally, those plants which dye black…

Blackberry Rubus fruticosus – *Young shoots, with salts of iron.*
Oak – Bark and acorns

How to hawk a heron

Hawks were most commonly used to hunt small prey such as rabbits, larks or pigeons (see page 71 for how to train a falcon) but Gage Earle Freeman, in his 1869 work *Practical Falconry*, describes how hawks could be used to hunt herons, a practice that was once common across Europe.

Herons are hawked on what is known as the 'passage;' …
the passing of herons from the trees on which they build to their frog or fishing grounds, and the passing back again. Falconers are stationed at convenient parts of this passage, down wind of the heronry, on the look-out for returning birds, which are called 'heavy', because they carry food; or some very daring man, with an excellent hawk, may even venture upon a tierce 'light' heron – i.e., one going out to fish; but this is difficult and dangerous. I need, perhaps, scarcely say that the falcon, and not the tierce [male falcon], is used for this flight.
 A quarter of a mile from the falconer, and a couple of hundred yards or so in the air, is the greatest distance a falconer ought to fly through – at any rate, as a rule. Herons have been killed with more law, but not often. Off go the hoods of two falcons when the heron, on his way home, has

*passed the falconer a little. He disgorges his fish, he turns
and goes down wind, making rings all the time in order to
get above the hawks. They make rings too, and larger ones
than his. One hawk is above the heron; she stoops, and hits
or misses; in either case perhaps, but certainly in the former,
both birds descend a little; but the second hawk has climbed
up and stoops in her turn. After some blows there is a catch,
both hawks 'bind' to the quarry, and all three come down
to the ground. Just before the ground is reached practised
hawks loose their hold to save the bump, but make in again
in a moment. You must ride at this sport, and that down
wind, as fast as you can ... if the heron is not hors de combat
when the falconer comes up, the neck must be seized, and
matters arranged as soon as possible. When heron hawks are
ridden to, as they always should be, the heron is often found
unhurt, or not seriously hurt· in that case, the hawks are fed
on hot pigeon, held under a dead heron's wing ... while the
heron is restored to liberty, to fight or fly another day.*

How to cure a head cold

According to *A New Herball* by William Turner (1551),
the following recipe will cure that most irritating of
ailments, the head cold.

*If the patient hath great heate in his head then make him
this: take a house leake and leaves of roses in like quantity,
well beaten and mixed with milk; stroke the same about
his temples. The same cooleth the blood and alayeth the
raging. Let him beware of strong drinks.*

If that doesn't do the trick and the head cold is really bothersome, then perhaps you might try this more extreme cure.

If a man becometh mad with cold, then it is good forth with to take a live black hen and cut open the same upon the back and lay her with blood and all upon the patient's head, for the same doth warm his head and brains very well.

How to prevent bad luck

Ancient Legends, Mystic Charms, and Superstitions of Ireland by Lady Wilde (1887) is full of mysterious and magical advice on how to protect the family from those most pesky of pests, witches and fairies.

The witches, however, make great efforts to steal the milk on May morning, and if they succeed, the luck passes from the family, and the milk and butter for the whole year will belong to the fairies. The best preventative is to scatter primroses on the threshold; and the old women tie bunches of primroses to the cows' tails, for the evil spirits cannot touch anything guarded by these flowers, if they are plucked before sunrise, not else. A piece of iron, also, made red hot, is placed upon the hearth; any old iron will do, the older the better, and branches of whitethorn and mountain ash are wreathed around the doorway for luck. The mountain ash has very great and mysterious qualities. If a branch of it be woven into the roof, that house is safe from fire for a year at least, and if a branch of it is mixed

*with the timber of a boat, no storm will upset it, and no
man in it be drowned for twelvemonth.*

How to restore a drowned person

This description of how to restore a drowned person from
A Shilling's Worth of Practical Receipts (1856) indicates
the rather lax attitude to water safety in Victorian times,
somehow conjuring up images of those taking a quiet Sunday
stroll along the river coming upon unfortunate urchins who
had tumbled into the river and required restoring.

*The greatest exertion should be used to take out the body
before the lapse of one hour, and the resuscitative process
should be immediately employed.*

*On taking bodies out of the Thames, ponds &c., the
following customs are to be used: −*
Never to be held up by the heels.
Not to be rolled on casks, or other rough usage.
Avoid the use of salt in all cases of apparent death.
*Particularly observe to do everything with the utmost
promptitude.*

For the drowned, attend to the following directions: −
*Convey the body, with the head raised, to the nearest
convenient house.*
Strip and dry the body: − clean the mouth and nostrils.
Young children: − between two persons in a warm bed.
*An Adult: − lay the body on a warm blanket, or bed, and in
cold weather, near the fire − in the warm season, air should
be freely admitted.*

It is to be gently rubbed with flannel, sprinkled with spirits, and a heated warming pan, covered, lightly moved over the back and spine.

To restore breathing: – Introduce the pipe of a pair of bellows (when no apparatus) into one nostril; close the mouth and the other nostril, then inflate the lungs, till the breast be a little raised; the mouth and nostrils must then be let free. Repeat this process till life appears.

Tobacco smoke is to be thrown gently up the fundament, with a proper instrument, or the bowl of a pipe covered so as to defend the mouth of the assistant.

The breast is to be fomented with hot spirits: – if no signs of life appear, the warm bath or hot brock &c., applied to the palms of the hands and soles of the feet.

Electricity early employed by a medical assistant.

The breath is the principal thing to be attended to.

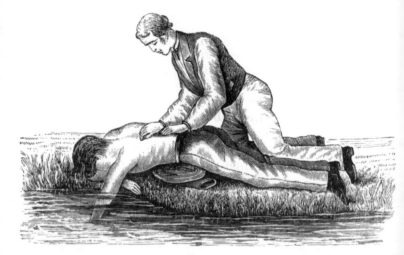

Although these instructions may have worked on Victorian urchins, they are not to be recommended for the modern victim of drowning, who would probably benefit from a trip to the hospital.

How to prevent tools from rusting

Rust is the enemy of every collector and keeper of tools, and *Every Man His Own Mechanic* (1886) contains the following advice on keeping rust at bay.

1. Boiled linseed oil will keep polished tools from rusting, if it is allowed to dry on them. Common sperm oil will prevent them from rusting for a short period. A coat of copal varnish is frequently applied to polished tools exposed to the weather. Woollen materials are the best wrappers for metals.
2. Iron and steel goods of all descriptions are kept free from rust by the following: – Dissolve ½ oz. of camphor in 1lb. of hog's lard, take off the scum and mix as much black lead as will give the mixture an iron colour. Iron and steel and machinery of all kinds rubbed over with this mixture and left with it on for twenty-four hours, and then rubbed with a linen cloth, will keep clean for months.

How to be a good man

Household Proverbs for Men (1863) advised that men should especially take heed of the following proverbs.

1. *Take care of the pence, and the pounds will take care of themselves.*
2. *A man is what a woman makes him.*
3. *He that goes a-borrowing, goes a-sorrowing.*
4. *He that serves God, serves a good master.*
5. *A cat in patterns catches no mice.*
6. *Waste not, want not.*
7. *Ill weeds grow apace.*
8. *Birds of a feather flock together.*
9. *Wilful waste makes woeful want.*
10. *Lightly come, lightly go.*
11. *God helps them who help themselves.*
12. *Right wrongs no man.*
13. *More are drowned in beer than in water.*
14. *Store is no sore.*
15. *When poverty comes in at the door, love flies out of the window.*
16. *Marry in haste and repent at leisure.*
17. *It is never too late to learn.*
18. *Fine feathers make fine birds.*
19. *Cleanliness is next to godliness.*
20. *It is better to cry over your goods than after them.*
21. *Well begun is half done.*
22. *Use the means and trust to God for the blessing.*
23. *There is no mirth good but with God.*
24. *Pay as you go, and keep from small score.*

How to prevent/cure flatulence

*To contain a certain amount of gas is natural to the
stomach and bowels; when this is in excess, then only does it
become inconvenient. And really the internal commotions
and noises – aptly to be compared to the thunder that
precedes a storm, and the convulsive movements that usher
in the earthquake – with which some persons are afflicted,
are most distressing, often rendering the unhappy sufferer
an object of dislike, if not of disgust.*

These wise words are from *Household Medicine and
Surgery, Sick-room Management and Cookery for Invalids*
(1854). The author goes on to further explain the
inconvenient effects of flatulence.

*The rumbling or gurgling sound in the bowels with which
some persons are annoyed – borborygmus – is produced by
gas passing from one part of the intestines to another, and
mixing with the contained fluids. This at all times produces
an annoying feeling of distention, and sometimes, pain,
amounting to that of colic.*

Modern medicine has offered no cure for this most
bothersome of issues, and we may do well to observe the
advice here given:

*Flatulence, whatever may be its extent, is generally
caused by dyspepsia, or torpid bowels, or by spasmodic
or permanent strictures of the intestines; it is also a usual
attendant upon fevers, colic, constipation and hysteria.*

When slight it may be removed by carminative medicines.
Gregory's mixture of rhubarb, magnesia, and ginger, a
tea-spoonful for a dose in a wine-glass of peppermint-
water, is very useful. Ginger-tea also is beneficial.
Stimulants also may be had recourse to, such as turpentine
in half-ounce doses, sal-volatile and Hoffman's anodyne; a
mixture of asafoetida and sulphuric ether, particularly in
hysterical females. Mild cathartics must be administered,
and exercise insisted upon. Great care must be bestowed
upon the diet, and all indigestible food avoided. Salads,
cabbage, cucumbers, and unripe fruits are peculiarly apt to
evolve gases even in a healthy stomach; and these therefore,
and also fermented liquors, should not be taken. Plain food,
with a little brandy-and-water, regular exercise, and the
avoidance of luxurious habits, will generally correct the
tendency to flatulence.

How to organise a funeral cortège

Notices Historical and Miscellaneous Concerning
Mourning Apparel (1850) includes a description of how a
typical Victorian funeral cortège might be arranged for a
member of the nobility.

It is not intended, in these few pages, to intrench upon
the province generally of the undertaker, whose onerous
business it is to take charge of all the arrangements on
those melancholy occasions when his services are required,
and to see the proper equipment of the procession to 'the
house appointed for all living' but, in recognition of the

manner of performing the last offices of the dead, as at present followed in this country, the following notice is given of the order of the cortège, as recently appropriated to the funeral of an English Earl: —

Four Mutes on horseback.

Two Cloakmen.

Plume of Feathers.

Two Cloakmen.

State horse, with a gentleman carrying the coronet of the deceased Earl on a crimson velvet cushion.

THE HEARSE

Drawn by six horses, and decorated with the emblazoned arms of the family.

Three mourning coaches: the first, with six horses, containing the sons (as chief mourners) and brothers of the deceased.

The second, containing his brothers-in-law.

The third, containing a brother-in-law and one of the executors of the deceased, with a friend.

Each mourning coach was escorted by four pages.

The private carriages of the deceased, and of several relatives and family closed the procession.

Although to the modern eye this may seem like a fairly elaborate funeral procession, the author then goes on to detail the astounding pageantry afforded to a celebrated politician of the Georgian era.

The following programme is given as that of a remarkable public funeral, ordered for a distinguished commoner, the

Right Hon. Charles James Fox, M.P. for Westminster, who died in 1806: –

Order of procession of the Funeral of the Right Hon. Charles James Fox, *from the Stable Yard, St James's, to Westminster Abbey, on Friday October 10th, 1806.*

Volunteer Cavalry

Six Marshallmen, two and two, with black scarves, silk hatbands and gloves.

High Constable of Westminster, on horseback, with black silk scarf, hatband and gloves.

Musicians playing solemn music.

Six Conductors, on foot, carrying black staves, covered with silk, and with silk hatbands and gloves.

Fifty-seven poor Men, in mourning cloaks,* with badge of the crest of the deceased, and with silk hatbands and gloves.

High Bailiff of Westminster, on horseback, with black silk scarf, hatband and gloves, supported by two Marshallmen, with silk hatbands and gloves.

High Steward of Westminster, in his carriage, with scarf, hatband and gloves.

Six Marshallmen, two and two, as before.

Musicians, playing the 'Dead March in Saul.'

Two Conductors on foot, with black staves &c., as before.

Gentlemen, Electors of Westminster, &c., in mourning cloaks, and with silk hatbands and gloves, four and four.

Deputation from the country, with black silk scarves, hatbands, and gloves.

Three Trumpets abreast.

*fifty-seven was the age of the deceased.

Black standard Banner, carried by a gentleman on horseback,
and with silk scarf, hatband, and gloves, supported by two
Gentlemen on foot, with scarves, hatbands and gloves.
Members of the Whig Club, in black mourning cloaks, and
in scarves, with silk hatbands and gloves, four and four.
Household, in mourning cloaks, with scarves, hatbands and
gloves, in two mourning coaches, with four horses.
Physicians and Medical Gentlemen, in black silk scarves,
hatbands and gloves, in two mourning coaches, with six
horses each.
Divines, in their gowns &c., with black silk scarves,
hatbands and gloves, in two mourning coaches with six
horses each.
Singing Boys of the Chapel Royal, in full dress, with black
silk scarves, hatbands and gloves.
Musicians playing solemn music.
Two Mutes on horseback, carrying staves, covered with
black silk, with silk hatbands and gloves.
State plume of Ostrich Feathers, with velvet falls, carried
by two men, with black silk scarves, hatbands and gloves,
supported by two pages with wands, scarves, hatbands
and gloves.
Two Mutes on horseback, as before.
Two men on horseback, in mourning cloaks, with black silk
hatbands and gloves.
The great Banner, carried by a Gentleman on horseback,
supported by two Gentlemen in mourning, with black silk
scarves, hatbands and gloves.
Two Horsemen in cloaks as before.
Two Bannerds, carried by Gentlemen on horseback, with
black silk scarves, hatbands and gloves.

Two Horsemen, as before.
Two Bannerds, as before.
Two Horsemen, as before.
Divines, in canonicals, with black silk scarves, hatbands,
and gloves, in a mourning coach with six horses.
The Crest of the Deceased, carried on a black velvet
cushion, by a Gentleman on horseback, uncovered, led by
two Grooms, with black silk scarves, hatbands and gloves.

THE HEARSE
Containing the Body, drawn by six state horses, led by
Grooms of Noblemen, with black silk scarves, hatbands
and gloves, attended by six Pages on each side, in deep
mourning, with truncheons, black silk scarves, hatbands
and gloves.
Six Noblemen, Pall-bearers, in full dress mourning, with
black silk scarves, hatbands, and gloves, in two mourning
coaches, with six horses each.
The Chief Mourner, with train cloak, and supported by
two Noblemen, with black silk scarves, hatbands, and
gloves, in a mourning coach with six horses.
Mr. Fox's private Secretary, Train-bearer to Chief
Mourner, with black silk scarf, hatband and gloves, in a
mourning coach with four horses.
The twenty Noblemen and Gentlemen Directors, part in
mourning coaches, and part walking, two by two.
A small black Banner, with the arms of the Deceased,
carried by Gentlemen on foot, with black silk scarf,
hatbands and gloves.
Peers, mourners, with black silk scarves, hatbands and
gloves, two by two, on foot.

Sons of Peers, mourners, as above.
Members of the House of Commons, mourners, with
scarves, as above.
Banner of Emblems, carried by a Gentleman on
horseback, with black silk scarf, hatband and gloves,
supported by two gentlemen on foot, with scarves &c.
Carriages of the Deceased and Relatives.
State Carriages.
Trumpets and Kettle Drums.
Volunteer Cavalry.

How to darn

There was a time when everyone knew how to darn, and people were happy to 'mend and make do' – rather than adopt the more modern model of 'bin and pop to the shops'. *Cassell's Home Encyclopedia* (1934) provides the following instructions.

Too heavy mending yarn pulls and strains the material to be darned, and soon leads to further holes; too fine a one only fills the rents with twice as much labour as is necessary, and does not last long. The idea is to counterfeit the weaving of the material, first one way and then the other, till the hole is filled with closely interlaced threads going over and under each other at right angles.

Start on sound material well outside the edges of the hole, running the needle (threaded double for all but small repairs) in and out of the stuff in a straight line. Return as close as possible to the first line, going under the stuff where that went over, and vice versa. At the end of each line do not pull thread tight, but leave a tiny loop. This allows for the shrinking of the new thread in the wash. Continue darning up and down till well outside the hole on the far side and on sound stuff again. Then darn closely across at right angles, alternately under and over the original lines of the stitches until the hole is completely filled. Thin places should never be allowed to run into holes. If they are darned one way only they will last for a long time.

How to get presented at Court

Getting presented at Court was vital for any young lady wishing to become part of the English social scene.

In fashionable Society a girl has no recognised position until she has been presented at Court ... The debutante is presented by her mother, or, if she should not have one, by some near relative. A bride is presented on her marriage, and usually by a near relative of her husband.

The methods have changed over the years, but *Complete Etiquette for Ladies and Gentlemen: A Guide to the Rules and Observances of Good Society* (1900) describes the Victorian method, in which girls had the opportunity to be presented to Queen Victoria four times a season (twice before Easter and twice after).

When a girl is about to be presented at Court she procures a large blank card, and write legibly upon it her own name and that of the lady who presents her, thus: 'Mrs. Percy, presented by Lady White' ... This card is left at the Lord Chamberlain's office in St. James's Palace at least two clear days before the drawing-room, and is accompanied by a note from the lady who is to present her ... The names are submitted for Her Majesty's approval, and on sending to the office two days later the lady receives two 'presentation' or pink cards, on which she write legibly the same words as those on the former card. These cards she takes with her to the palace, one being left with the page-in-waiting at the top of the grand staircase; the other is taken by an official at the door of the presence-chamber, and passed to the Lord Chamberlain, who reads the name to Her Majesty.

The doors of the Palace are opened at two o'clock, and the Queen enters the throne room at three. Ladies carry their trains, folded, over the arm until they reach the door of the picture gallery, where it is removed from its wearer's arm by the attendants in waiting, and the lady passes across the gallery with it flowing at full length to the door of the throne-room.

If the lady is to be presented she must have her right hand ungloved, and as she bends before the Queen she extends her hands palm downwards; the Queen places her hand upon it, the lady touches the royal hand with her lips, and the presentation is over; the lady passes on, stepping backwards, curtseying to those members of the royal family present.

A lady requires to be re-presented when any change occurs in her social status. For instance, she must be again presented on her marriage, if she has been presented *before, also should her husband succeed to any higher title. If she fails in this, she has no further right to appear at Court.*

The book goes on to discuss the correct clothing to be worn on such an occasion.

The question of dress is an important matter at a Drawing-room. Only full dress (low bodice and short sleeves) is admissible … A Court train is also de rigueur and should be from three to four yards long, according to the height of the wearer … The other imperative portions of a Court costume are the plume and lappets.* There was at one time an inclination to wear coloured feathers; but these are not strictly Court dress, and are regarded unfavourably in high quarters. The white plume is correct, and may be arranged according to taste: it is generally arranged on the left side, and the lappets on the right. Those ladies who possess lappets will find them much more graceful and becoming than a tulle veil, though the latter is quite correct, and may be worn if preferred. The hair may be arranged according to taste, and flowers, ribbons or jewels worn in it or not.

White is the regulation colour for a debutante's gown, also for a lady being presented on her marriage, unless her age is such as to make so youthful a style undesirable.

---

* Lappets were two lengths of material attached to a headdress, such as a bishop's mitre, that generally adorned ladies' headgear in the early twentieth century.

How to make ginger wine

The following recipe for making homemade ginger wine can be found in *Household Management* by 'An Old Housekeeper' (1877).

Dissolve fifteen pounds of loaf-sugar in ten gallons of water, into which put the beaten whites of twelve eggs; mix this well, and boil and skim it; then put in twelve ounces of Jamaica ginger, peeled and bruised; boil the whole for half an hour in a covered vessel, then pour it into a tub, and when nearly cold, put into it a glassful of fresh yeast. Let it ferment three days, and on the second add the thin peel of four Seville oranges and six lemons: cask it, and bottle it in six weeks. Ginger wine should be well corked; and the corks should be tied or wired down. The colour may be improved by adding a table-spoonful of burnt sugar, first mixed with some of the liquor, when the cask is filled up.

How to skin a lion

First, catch your lion (see page 13). According to Rowland Ward's *Sportsman's Handbook* (1923), essential skinning apparatus is as follows.

1. Forceps 2. Chain-hooks 3. Scissors 4. Brain-scoop 5. Scalpel 6. Blowpipe 7. Scissors

The minimum apparatus required to skin an animal in the field is a knife, a small saw, a pair of pliers and some cutting pincers (and, of course, a strong stomach). Ward notes that 'A tiger, for instance, can be perfectly well-skinned by a skilful hand with an ordinary knife, costing only a few shillings.' Ward then advises that before any cuts are made the hunter should thoroughly inspect their booty.

Directly a specimen is secured, inspect the eye and nose, and make concise memorandum of its colour and any peculiarity of its appearance. A note should also be taken of the colour on the bills, legs etc., of birds (the brilliancy of which may fade), and particular mention should be recorded of the eyelids, and, if they have any, their colour. The same may be said with regard to wattles and other areas of naked skin, because, when these parts dry, the colours not only fade, but absolutely change, so that the taxidermist at home may be led to a wrong conclusion.

The hunter need then only wait for the carcass to cool somewhat before beginning the task of skinning the beast.

Should it be desired to preserve the entire skin of a large animal, it must without delay first be turned on its back, and a cut can then be made down the centre of the underside of the body from the chest to the tip of the tail … The skin should be taken off cleanly without any flesh or fat adhering to it, because flesh or fat in a hot climate soon goes bad and taints the skin, and then the hair on the spot falls out … One cut from the centre of the chest to the tail, together with smaller one at the back of the head to remove the skull, is sufficient, the skin of the limbs and the

*neck being turned inside out and afterwards dried with a
little stuffing of tow or dried grass.*

Should the hunter also wish to preserve the lion's skull as
a trophy, Charles McCann advises the following method in
his 1927 *A Shikari's Pocket-book.*

*Cut off all the removable flesh. Take out the brain through
the orifice at the back by pushing a stick into it and stirring
them up, then shaking out the resultant porridge. Pouring
hot water into the brain-case and shaking it out again will
help greatly to bring away the contents. Do not give this
job to an ignorant native to do, unless he has done it before
correctly in your presence. If not he will inevitably chop
off the back of the skull with an axe in order to get at the*

*brains. Wash the skull and hang it up to dry, after tying the
lower jawbone firmly on to it.*

Ward cautions that certain care must be taken when skinning
a big cat if you want the trophy to resemble anything like
the beast in life. (Most people have had the unfortunate
experience of encountering bad taxidermy at a provincial
museum or curio shop and can agree it is not a happy sight.)

*With tigers, lions, leopards, etc., the ears, lips, paws, and
nose need special care. The ears should be skinned as
close to the skull as possible, as the cartilage of the ears
is required if the head is afterwards mounted. The ears
should be carefully skinned so that they form bags, and the
fingers can be inserted inside as far as the tips of the ears.
This admits of air getting to the ears and drying them
quickly before there is any chance of putrefaction setting
in. The lips should also be skinned so that they can be
turned inside out, but care must be taken that all the black
portion of the lip remains on the skin, otherwise there
will be difficulty afterwards when the head is mounted in
providing proper lips. Having skinned the lips so that they
can be turned inside out, be careful to remove all the flesh
from inside where the whiskers have their roots, and make
a few cuts with a knife between the rows of whiskers to put
the preservative in. If any flesh is left here it is certain to
go bad before the skin dries, and the hair will then slip, i.e.
fall away. The spongy fatty substance inside the pads of
the feet should be cut away, for this also takes long to dry,
and in a hot climate decomposition sets in before it can dry.*

The skin is now ready to be pinned out to dry.

After having freed them from all meat and gristle, rub a mixture of equal parts salt and powdered alum over all parts of the skin, especially round the eyes and nostrils, lower lip, and both the inside and outside of the ears; then put the skins out to dry in the shade – keeping the face part open at first with sticks – so as to allow air to circulate through them, gradually drying them quite flat by putting stones on them at night

At this point it might be wise to listen to the advice of Brigadier General R. Pigot in *Twenty-five Years Big Game Hunting* (1928).

In pegging out a tiger or a lion skin it is more than ever important to preserve the natural shape of the skin. It is easy to stretch such a skin lengthways and thereby increase the measurement of it but stretching it in length will decrease the breadth and completely destroy the look of the trophy.

And there you have it, the skin of a lion with which to adorn your hunting lodge and impress your neighbours.

How to become a pigeon fancier

The New and Complete Pigeon Fancier (1830) describes the attraction of keeping and breeding pigeons.

The beautiful varieties of tame pigeon are so numerous,

that it would be a fruitless attempt to describe them all; for human art has so much altered the colour and figure of this bird, that pigeon fanciers, by pairing male and female of different sorts, can, as they express it, breed them to a feather.

Once you have fallen under the spell of the pigeon and have decided to keep some birds, the first job is to build a dovecote in which to house them.

In the first place, it is necessary to seek for a convenient situation, of which none can be better adapted to the purpose than the centre of a spacious court or farm-yard, for pigeons being naturally timorous the least noise affrights them; therefore, it is not without reason, that pigeon houses are generally erected at a proper distance from the rustling noise of trees shaken by high winds, and the load roarings of mill-dams.

With to regard to the size of the pigeon-house, it depends entirely on the number of birds intended to be kept: but it is better to have it roomy, than to be pinched for want of it; and as to the form of it, the round are preferable to the square ones; because it will not be so easy for the rats to come at them in the former as in the latter.

In order to prevent rats from getting in the pigeon-house, by climbing up the side, the walls should be sheathed with plates of tin, for about two feet in height and project out three or four inches at the top, which should be pointed with sharp wire, to prevent their clambering any higher; also the outside angles of a square pigeon-house ought to be particularly guarded against the devastations of these formidable enemies to the pigeon tribe.

The covering of a pigeon-house should be well put together, so that not the least rain may penetrate through it. The whole building must be covered with hard plaster, and white-washed within and without; white being the colour pigeons most delight in, and because the building is easier discerned by the bird when at a distance, from its white appearance. As pigeon's dung is very corrosive, care should be taken that the foundation is well laid, the flooring good and the whole building well cemented. It should be a standing rule, that there be no door or other aperture towards the east; these should always face the south, pigeons being very fond of the sun, especially in winter; but if the window of the pigeon house faces the north, it should never be opened but in very warm weather, when the air may have free admittance, which, at that season of the year, is both refreshing and wholesome to the pigeon.

The pigeon house must have a cincture, made either of free-stone or parget, reaching from the projecture under the window to nearly the middle of the pigeon house; the use of which is for the birds to rest upon when they come out of the fields; and at this aperture should be fixed a portcullis, or sliding blind, the sides of which must be well lined with tin, fenced with sharp-pointed wire, strongly fastened to the wall, as a barrier against the rats. This portcullis or sliding blind, may be drawn up at pleasure, by means of a cord and pulley, properly fixed to it, and the pigeon set at liberty, or confined, as inclination may dictate, or occasion require.

The nests or coves, in a pigeon-house generally consist of long square holes made in the walls, and these are so

contrived, that the pigeon sits dark, which is a situation
they much covet when hatching … As the pigeon does not
always build a nest, it is necessary to have a small cavity
sunk at the bottom of the coves to prevent the eggs from
rolling aside; for, though the pigeon may sit well in her
nest, if this accident happens they will certainly be spoiled:
particular care should also be taken, that the coves in the
walls be of a size sufficient for the cock and hen to stand in.
The first range of nests should be about four feet from the
ground. These nests or coves must be placed in a quincunx
[the shape of the five pips on the fifth side of a die] order,
or chequer-wise, and not directly over one another; nor
should they be raised any higher than within one yard of
the top of the wall. Before the mouth of every cover, which
must be built even with the wall, should be fixed a small
flat stone, to project out of the wall three or four inches, for
the pigeons to rest upon in going in, or coming out from
their nests, or when the weather obliges them to remain
prisoners at home.

Once the dovecote has been constructed, the pigeon-
fancier may next go about stocking it with birds.

The dove-cot, or common blue-pigeon, being both prolific
and hardy, is most worthy the attention of country-people,
as it is generally remarked, that the small pigeons rear
the greatest number of young ones; but when the breed
of pigeon proves too small, it will be proper to intermix
with the dove-cot a few of the common tame sort; in the
procuring of which, care must be taken not to select those
of glaring colours, for the others will not easily associate

with them. Others recommend the dark grey-coloured pigeon, inkling to ash-colour and black; especially if she has some redness in her eyes, and a ring of gold-colour about her neck; which, according to the judgement of some, are never failing signs of her fertility.

Pigeons usually take rest at noon, and as it agrees with them, they should not be disturbed; morning and evening are the best times for giving them their food. Be mindful also that they are plentifully supplied with water, that they be kept free from vermin; that the pigeon house be kept clean and frequently strewed with gravel: these rules properly observed will greatly increase your stock.

In order to fatten young pigeons for the table in winter, take them before they can fly, when they are stout birds, and pull the largest quill-feathers out of their wings, which will confine them to their nests; and the substance of the nourishment they receive, not being diffused for want of exercise, soon fattens them.

Farmers, for their own sakes, should be careful that the pigeon house is kept clean, and the dung preserved; it being the finest manure in the world, and claims precedence of the dung of all other animals. It is enuded with a nitrous quality, and is of a very hot nature, which makes it an excellent soil for cold, moist, damp grounds.

There are also some useful tips for distinguishing between the male and female birds.

1. The cock has always a longer and stouter breast bone than the hen.
2. His head and cheeks are broader and fuller, and he has a

bolder look than the hen.
3. The vent in the hen, and the bone near the vent, is always
more open than in the cock.
4. In young pigeons, that which squeaks longest in the nest
generally proves to be a hen; and when there are two in the
nest, the largest usually turns out to be the cock.
5. The coo of the cock is longer, a great deal louder, and
more masculine than the hens; and the cock often makes
a half round in his playing, which the hen seldom does,
though a warm lively hen will sometimes show, and play
very like a cock, and when lecherous will even attempt to
tread another pigeon.

The author goes on to warn that pigeons can be easily tempted away by rival dovecotes. Should their heads be turned by a more luxurious home or more sumptuous food, the author recommends the following tips to ensure that the pigeons remain happy and loyal to their own dovecote.

Take the head and feet of a gelt goat, boil them until the
flesh parts from the bone: take this flesh and boil it again in
the same liquor till the whole is reduced to a jelly; then put
in some clean potter's earth, and knead the whole together
to the consistency of dough, which make into small loaves,
and dry them in the sun or oven, but be careful they are
not burned: when they are dry, place them in the most
convenient parts of the pigeon-house, when the pigeons will
soon peck at it, and liking the taste, will not leave it but
with regret. Some make use of goat's head boiled in urine,
with a mixture of salt, cumin and hemp.

How to treat a bee sting

The Bee-Master's Companion and Assistant by James
Bonner (1789) offers advice on how to treat a bee sting.

*As we now go forward to handle Bees, it becomes us
therefore to guard ourselves against their stings. In the
first place, Bees seldom use their stings, unless provoked
or affronted; therefore you must beware of giving them
the least offence, for they will hazard their lives rather
than let an affront pass unresented: for exasperate them
near their hives, you may as well take a lion by the beard,
or a bear by the tooth, as offer to capitulate with them: in
such a case the only thing to be done is presently to scour
off, and shelter yourselves within doors, and peep out at
them, till once their fury be abated, and the remembrance
of their affront be obliterated; then you may renew your
acquaintance with them, and if you come in an humble
manner, and walk gently and submissively among them,
then they will use you very friendly.*

*In all things you have to do with Bees, do it in a soft,
calm, gentle, and submissive manner; come not among
them in a rash hasty manner; neither must you come
puffing and blowing, nor with bad smells about you. Come
to them in the same manner you would appear before your
patron, when you want a favour at his hand.*

*When Bees are offended at a person, the chief part they
aim at to wound him in is the face and hands, being the
places they know are most vulnerable. But in case those
places be covered, and proof against them, then they will
surround him all about, in order to see if they can spy any*

unguarded place in his coverings, any aperture or crevice about his shirt, hands, breeches, knees, &c. and if they find the least opening in any of them, they will push in at it, and so leave their sting, and very life, behind.

There have been many remedies prescribed (to little purpose) to cure the wound received by a sting. Oil of olives, or any mild oil is thought by many to be a cure; bruised parsley gives ease, say some; the honey taken out of the Bee that inflicted the wound is thought a good cure; the sweet spirit of vitriol well rubbed in the wound will prevent pain or swelling ... Repeated experiments oft shew that the ease received from any of the above remedies is but seldom, and may rather be imputed to an accident than a cure; yet I make no doubt they may give ease sometimes.

The sting and poison is ejected in a moment, and pain and swelling take place the same instant, when the cure is often far to seek and ill to find. The moment I receive a sting, I pull it out, and takes a kail dock, ash, or almost any green leaf which is soonest got, and is always at hand, and bruises it a little, and rubs it in the wound. Sometimes, if near water, I wash the wound, or apply a wet and cold cloth to it, and have thought it sometimes gave me a little ease; but it is not one in a dozen I apply any remedy to at all, for it seldom makes me uneasy, and I know a little patience and time compounded together will make an effectual cure.

How to make barley water

Barley water conjures up comforting images of hot summer days and watching Wimbledon, and here *Cassell's*

Home Encyclopedia (1934) describes how you can make your own.

Wash 2 tablespoonfuls of pearl barley in cold water, put it into a saucepan with two pints of cold water, bring to the boil and boil gently till the liquid is reduced to 1 pint. Strain, and sweeten or salt according to taste. One cupful of this, added to one cupful of milk, hot or cold makes a pleasant invalid drink.

For large quantities of barley water as a wholesome drink make as above, adding to every pint, while hot, the juice of half a lemon and one tablespoon of sugar. Barley water should be freshly made each day, and kept in a cool place.

How to make a tent

Those making up their minds to become campers must be prepared to exercise their faculties for promptness, order, self-reliance, and resourcefulness, as there is no other vocation that calls so much for all the best that is in oneself.

So advises W. J. Pearce in his paean to camping, *Fixed and Cycle Camping* (1909). Pearce goes on to describe how to make one of the most popular styles of tent.

We now come to a very popular tent, which may in time become almost universal ... [it] is called the 'Canadian'.

Two widths of material will give a tent 6 feet long, but to be really comfortable I prefer 6 feet 6 inches. This tent has a wall, which is a decided advantage, whilst the eaves carry the water clear of the tent walls and keep the ground drier. Decide upon which height, length and width, draw this to scale, allowing 1 foot 9 inches to 2 feet for the walls. Calculate the amount of material for the roof, carrying it well down to within 6 or 9 inches of the ground, allowing for the eaves to be at least 15 inches deep. I am a firm believer in having the roof come as near the ground as possible; rain cannot reach the walls, neither can the wind get under the eaves so easily. From the first I determined upon this, and am pleased that experts have received it with approval and adopted it … In this case the roof comes to within 6 inches of the ground, giving a very rakish appearance to the tent. Above all things, when cutting out the doors do not forget to add the extra height of the wall to the 6 inch curtain end shown in the diagram.

Having sewn the roofing, cut triangular pieces, not round, for the eyelet supports, and sew two pieces under the hem, where the eyelets are to be placed, usually three or four along each side of the eaves, one of course at each corner. If your wall is to be 1 foot 9 inches or 2 feet deep, add 6 inches to this for the curtain. The walls are made from the same material as the doors, and along the bottom put in holes or eyelets for the loops. Two pieces of Lawn* must be sewn inside the doors and walls where they join the eaves as a support, and to take the strain which is put upon these four points.

If three widths of material are used for the roof, this will allow the 6 feet 6 inch tent and hood at both ends. The hood screens the door from the rain and wind and allows cooking to be done under cover outside the tent … Tents

*made in this design and material will stand the wind and
keep out the rain. My 'Giant Canadian' will sleep six or
seven in comfort.*

* Made from Egyptian cotton.

The tent being made, Pearce gives the following advice on
how to find a decent spot to pitch the tent.

*The fundamentals of a good camp site are convenience for
obtaining water, shelter from the wind by pitching the tent
near, but not under, hedges and trees, smooth ground, near
a river or the sea if possible, freedom from disturbance or
inconvenience by cattle, nearness to a farm for obtaining
butter, eggs and milk. It should not be too far from the
station, accessible, dry, have bathing accommodation, and
if for week-ends should not be too far from home.*

Once the site has been selected, the camper must next
pitch their tent.

*Having arrived at your destination, full of the excitement
born of a new experience ... the first thing to attend to
is 'Tent Pitching.' To do this, unroll the tent and spread
it to its fullest extent upon the grass, door uppermost. Be
careful that the pole is placed well and securely into the
pole seating. The poleman should be assisted to raise the
tent and remain steady whilst the remainder each secure
a red runner; failing these distinctive marks, four at equal
distance around the tent. Previous to this the pegs should
have been laid in a circle, the diameter of which must be*

about eight yards, ready for picking up. See that the door is facing away from the wind, drive in four pegs at the required distance and secure the guy ropes over them. Lace up the door, hook over the wall, and proceed to peg out the remaining guys, making sure that the tent is assuming a symmetrical appearance. Whilst others are unpacking, one should continue pegging down the wall ... The tent should be tight; no sagging allowed.

Once the tent is erected, the campers may begin to enjoy their sojourn outdoors.

The arrival and tent pitching having been described, the first meal, usually tea, is discussed, and probably a quiet chat and smoke enjoyed before the final touches are put to the tent arrangements, and preparations for the first night's rest. The turning in for the first night is always an exciting and sometimes anxious moment. Providing the tent is pitched securely no fear need be occasioned in this direction. It may be assumed that little or no sleep will come to the eyes of the tyro until the morning, and usually an early turn out takes place after the restless hours that have passed. But all this will shape itself after two or three days, when one become entirely oblivious to his surroundings and sleeps the sleep of the just – sound and long.

How to dress like a gentleman

Some tips become quickly outmoded, but these tips for the stylish man from *All About Etiquette: or The Manners of*

Polite Society for Ladies, Gentlemen, and Families (1879)
are timeless.

*Among the best dressed men on the continent, as well as
in England, black, though not confined to the clergy, is
now (excepting for dinner and evening dress) in much
less general use than formerly. They adopt the darker
shades of blue and brown; and for undress, almost as great
diversity of colours as of fabrics.*

*If you wear your beard, wear it in moderation
– extremes are always vulgar. Avoid all fantastic
arrangements of the hair, either turning it under in a
roll, or allowing it to straggle in long and often seemingly
'uncombed and unkempt' masses over the coat collar,
or having it cropped so close as to give the wearer the
appearance of a sporting character.*

*For appendages, eschew all flash stones; nothing is more
unexceptionable for sleeve-buttons and the fastenings of
the front of a shirt than fine gold, fashioned in some simple
form, sufficiently massive to indicate use and durability, and
skilfully and handsomely wrought, if ornamented at all.
A gentleman carries a watch for convenience and secures it
safely upon his person, wearing it with no useless ornament
paraded to the eye. It is like his pencil and purse, good of
its kind, and, if he can afford it, handsome, but it is never
flashy. The fashion for wearing signet rings is not so general,
perhaps, as it was a little while since, but it still retains a place
among the minutiae of the present subject. Here, again,
the same rules of good taste apply as to other ornaments.
When worn at all, everything of this sort should be most
unexceptionally and unmistakably tasteful and genuine.*

How to catch and preserve eels

Eels were once plentiful in the rivers of Britain, and as such were the mainstay of British cuisine. Eel pie, jellied eels, and eel and mash were all popular dishes. Though it has now fallen out of fashion, *The Sportsman's Directory and Park and Gamekeeper's Companion* by John Mayer (1838) recommends this technique for catching and preserving eels.

To take eels, there should be traps or brays at the heads of the ponds to receive them when they run in heavy showers or pots filled with sheep's entrails, and sunk. In marsh ditches, use a net about twelve feet long in the cod, and nine feet wide; put three hoops of different sizes into the cod. To keep it open; corks and heavy leads in front, with a cord at each end to draw it up by. Take distances, about twenty yards at a time, first taking the eels out. When you find they strike into the mud, use spears.

To make a reserve of them, when taken, have a bricked cistern, three feet deep, that is fed by a running stream; put them into it, make a fagot with small round wood, and tie both ends with small chains: have another fastened to each of them, giving it length enough for the middle to reach near the curb of the cistern, where have a hook fixed to hang it upon. The eels will draw into the fagot, and by pulling it out quickly, you may suit yourself with a dish at pleasure.

How to survive a long sea voyage

In the days before air travel it was not uncommon for keen travellers to spend a good deal of time at sea. For example, in 1833 it would take a steam ship 22 days to sail from England to America, and it could take as long as four months to sail to Australia. *Out at Sea; or, The Emigrant Afloat* by P. B. Chadfield (1862) contains a plethora of advice for the sea traveller.

It has often been remarked that in no phase or condition of society is the human character more strongly developed than on board ship. The idle become more idle, the selfish more selfish, and the disagreeable still more disagreeable. The explanation is simple: all have their temper and patience severely tried by the various annoyances and inconveniences unavoidable from so many human creatures being crowded within the narrow limits of even a commodious vessel.

According to the rules of the ship the passengers should rise at seven o'clock in the morning, and retire to rest at ten o'clock in the evening, at which hour all lights in the berth should be put out ... The only circumstances that warrant a breach of the rule respecting going to bed at ten o'clock are, when during hot weather, rain or other causes prevent proper ventilation of the between-decks, in which case many persons very naturally feel a repugnance to the close atmosphere of their berths.

Chadfield goes on to describe how meals were organised aboard.

The occupants of each portion of a vessel are usually divided into messes of about eight adults, for the purpose of cooking, eating their meals, and drawing their rations. These little communities have each a captain or managing man, selected from amongst themselves by the purser, for the purpose of looking after the interests of his mess.

It will be seen, by reference to the list of rations, there would be, for a mess of eight adults in the steerage, 8 lbs. preserved meat, 10 lbs. of salt beef, and 8 lbs. of salt pork. This would, with the other rations, supply the following bill of fare: –

SUNDAY – 3 lbs. preserved meat, and suet pudding with raisins.

MONDAY – 4lbs. pork, and pea soup.

TUESDAY – 5 lbs. beef, and preserved potatoes.

WEDNESDAY – 2 lbs. preserved meat, boiled rice, and suet pudding.

THURSDAY – 4 lbs. pork, and pea soup.

FRIDAY – 3 lbs. preserved meat, and rice.

SATURDAY – 5 lbs. beef, and potatoes.

Hot water is provided by the cook at eight o'clock in the morning and five o'clock in the afternoon, for making tea or coffee. Oatmeal porridge, or burgoo, is useful as an occasional substitute for breakfast.

This may not appear a very sumptuous table to any person unaccustomed to the sea; but it must be remembered that there is not much exercise on board ship, and therefore less food is required than on shore.

To conclude his advice on eating aboard ship, Chadfield provides this delightful recipe for what he calls 'Sea Pie.'

*Sea Pie may be made in two ways. One is to put a layer
of potatoes, and a few slices of onions, at the bottom of a
saucepan; then a layer of cooked meat, with a thin crust
over it, not forgetting to leave a hole in the middle for a
'hatchway' as seaman call it; then repeat the layers of meat
and potatoes, and cover with a thin crust as before. This is a
'two-decker', when a 'three-decker' is required, add another
layer of each kind, and another crust. Pour in sufficient
water to cover the topmost layer of potatoes, and boil till
the potatoes are nicely done.*

*Another plan is to mix all the ingredients together, and
cut up the paste, rolled very thin, into small pieces, and place
at the top; then boil all up together till the potatoes are done.
This is much the simplest plan, and quite as good as the other.*

How to ride side-saddle

*One day, in the middle of February 1880, a goodly
company, comprising many thousands of persons, assembled
upon the lawn of a nobleman's residence in the vicinity of
Dublin; ostensibly for the purpose of hunting, but in reality
to gaze at and chronicle the doings of a very distinguished
foreign lady, who had lately come to our shores.*

*There is for me so great an attraction in a number of
'ladies on horseback' that I looked at them, and at them
alone. One sees gentlemen riders every hour in the day, but
ladies comparatively seldom; every hunting morning finds
about a hundred and fifty mounted males ready for the
start, and only on average about six females, of whom not
more than half will ride to hounds.*

On the day of which I write, however, ladies on horseback were by no means uncommon: I should say there were at least two hundred present upon the lawn. Some rode so well, and were so beautifully turned out, that the most hypercritical could find no fault; but of the majority – what can I say? Alas! Nothing would sound at all favourable. Such horses, such saddles, such rusty bridles, such riding-habits, such hats, whips and gloves; and, above all, such coiffures! My very soul was sorry.

So we are introduced to the fabulously monikered Mrs Power O'Donoghue, who in her 1889 book *Ladies on Horseback* allows us a glimpse into what it was like to be a lady rider in the Victorian era. After so colourfully setting the scene, O'Donoghue goes on to give her advice on how to learn to ride side-saddle.

I conceive it to be an admirable plan to learn to ride without a stirrup at all. Of course I do not mean that a lady should ever go out park-riding or hunting sans the aid of such an appendage, but she should be taught the necessity of dispensing with it in case of emergency. The benefits arising from such training are manifold. First, it imparts a freedom and independence which cannot otherwise be acquired; secondly, it gives an admirable and sure seat over fences; thirdly, it is an excellent means of learning how to ride from balance; and fourthly, in spite of its apparent difficulties, it is in the end a mighty simplifier, inasmuch as, when the use of the stirrup is again permitted, all seems such marvellously plain sailing, that every obstacle seems to vanish from the learner's path.

To sit erect upon your saddle is a point of great importance; if you acquire a habit of stooping it will grow upon you, and it is not only a great disfigurement, but not unfrequently the cause of serious accident, for if the horse suddenly throws up his head, he hits you upon the nose, and deprives you of more blood than you may be able to replace in a good while.

As soon as you can feel yourself quite at home upon your mount, and have become accustomed to its walking motion, your attendant will urge him into a gentle trot. And now prepare yourself for the beginning of sorrows. Your first sensations will be that of being shaken to pieces. You are, of course, yet quite ignorant of the art of rising in your saddle, and the trot of the horse fairly churns you. Your hat shakes, your hair flaps, your elbows bang to your sides, you are altogether miserable. Still you hold on bravely, though you are ready to cry from the horrors of the situation.

Your attendant, by way of relieving you, changes the trot to a canter, and then you are suddenly transported to Elysium. The motion is heavenly. You have nothing to do but sit close to your saddle, and you are borne delightfully along. It is too ecstatic to last. Alas! It will never teach you to ride, and so you return to the trot and the shaking and

the jogging, the horrors of which are worse than anything
you have previously experienced. You try vainly to give
yourself some ease, but fail utterly, and at length dismount
— hot, tired, and disheartened.

O'Donoghue does not mince her words and indicates
that it is a long journey from the beginner to the stylish,
composed side-saddle expert. She leaves us with another
essential tip for what to do if the horse bolts.

In the event of a horse running away, you must of course
be guided by circumstances and surroundings, but my
advice always is, if you have a fair road before you, let
him go. Do not attempt to hold him in, for the support
which you afford him with the bridle only helps the
mischief. Leave his head quite loose, and when you feel
him beginning to tire — which he will do soon without the
support of the rein — flog him until he is ready to stand
still. I warrant that a horse treated thus, especially if you
can breast him up hill, will rarely run away a second time.
He never forgets his punishment, nor seeks to put himself
in for repetition of it.

How to preserve poultry

Before home freezers became the norm, food was preserved
by bottling or canning. Cyril Grange, in his 1949 *The*
Complete Book of Home Food Preservation, recommends
the following methods to preserve your excess fowls.

*In the majority of cases, poultry will be in the greatest
need of preserving because so many fowls are kept and
there is bound to come a period when there is more poultry
to dispose of than a household can possibly eat at one time.*

*Preparing and cooking. Absolute freshness and
cleanliness is essential, especially with fish. Remove large
bones to make the pack economical and prepare and
cook as if preparing for table except that the meats, etc.,
should NOT be cooked until fully tender. The sterilizing
completes the cooking … Do not pack raw meats, etc. Add
the necessary seasoning during cooking, not in the can. Do
not use flour on the meat, etc.*

*Roasting brings out the best flavour but boiling is
sometimes preferable and has of course a flavour of its
own. Old hens are best boiled or steamed; tender chicken
roasted. Turkeys, geese and ducks should be roasted. Fish
may be boiled, baked or fried.*

*Cook as for table, endeavouring to preserve or induce as
much flavour as possible.*

*When the meat is cooked to the proper degree it is
packed while hot into heated bottles or cans. These bottles
must be heated, otherwise if cold, the sudden contact with
the hot meat would cause them to crack.*

*The meat, etc., should be cut quickly into pieces which
will pass through the neck of the bottle. No piece of meat
must touch the top of the bottle or can or lids because the
grease may cause difficulty with sealing.*

*A 3 to 3½lb chicken cooked and cut up will fill a quart
bottle … A small chicken may be bottled whole, trussed
up tightly, but larger ones should be cut up into convenient
pieces so that each is packed in with the other. It is*

preferable for home use to pack all poultry cut up, or space is wasted to an extraordinary extent.

As each container is packed, a covering liquid is poured in to within ½ inch of the top just to cover.

This covering liquid is hot stock … the hot stock should be strained, allowed to cool, the fat removed and then heated up again to boiling point, when it will be ready for putting into bottles.

[To sterilize] Cook in a pressure cooker (60 minutes for a whole chicken).

How to use the English method of fortune-telling by cards

A Handbook of Cartomancy: Fortune-telling and Occult Divination by Grand Orient (1889) reveals the secrets of fortune-telling with cards.

In Fortune-Telling by Cards – as in all games in which they are employed – the Ace ranks highest in value. Then comes the King, followed by the Queen, Knave, Ten, Nine, Eight, and Seven, with the other numbers in their order.

The comparative value of the different suits is as follows: – First on the list stands Clubs, as they mostly portend happiness, and, no matter how numerous, or how accompanied, are rarely or never of bad augury. Next come Hearts, which usually signify joy, liberality, or good temper. Diamonds, on the contrary, denote delay, quarrels, and annoyance, while Spades, the worst of all, signify grief, sickness and loss of money.

We are, of course, speaking generally, as, in many cases, the position of the cards entirely changes their signification, their individual and relative meaning being often widely different. Thus, for example, the King of Hearts, the Nine of Hearts, and the Nine of Clubs respectively signify a liberal man, joy, and success in love; but change their position by placing the King between the two nines, and you would read that a man, then rich and happy, would ere long be consigned to prison.

The meanings of the cards are as follows.

Ace of Clubs – Wealth, happiness, and peace of mind.
King of Clubs – A dark man, upright, faithful, and affectionate in disposition.
Queen of Clubs – A dark woman, gentle and pleasing.
Knave of Clubs – A sincere but hasty friend. Also a dark man's thoughts.
Ten of Clubs – Unexpected riches, and loss of a dear friend.
Nine of Clubs – Disobedience to friends' wishes.
Eight of Clubs – A covetous man. Also warns against speculations.
Seven of Clubs – Promises good fortune and happiness, but bids a person beware of the opposite sex.
Six of Clubs – Predicts a lucrative business.
Five of Clubs – A prudent marriage.
Four of clubs – Cautiousness against inconstancy or change of object for the sake of money.
Three of Clubs – Shews that a person will be more than once married.

Two of Clubs – A disappointment.
Ace of Diamonds – A letter – from whom, and what about,
must be judged from neighbouring cards.
King of Diamonds – A fair man, hot tempered, obstinate
and revengeful.
Queen of Diamonds – A fair woman, fond of company
and a coquette.
Knave of Diamonds – A near relation who considers only
his interests. Also a fair person's thoughts.
Ten of Diamonds – Money.
Nine of Diamonds – Shews that a person is fond of roving.
Eight of Diamonds – A marriage late in life.
Seven of Diamonds – Satire, evil speaking.
Six of Diamonds – Early marriage and widowhood.
Five of Diamonds – Unexpected news.
Four of Diamonds – Trouble arising from unfaithful
friends; also a betrayed secret.
Three of Diamonds – Quarrels, law-suits, and domestic
disagreements.
Two of Diamonds – An engagement against the wishes of
friends.
Ace of Hearts – The house. If attended by Spades,
it foretells quarrelling – if by Hearts, affections and
friendship – if by diamonds, money and distant friends –
if by clubs, feasting and merry-making.
King of Hearts – A fair man, of good-natured disposition,
but hasty and rash.
Queen of Hearts – A fair woman, faithful, prudent, and
affectionate.
Knave of Hearts – The dearest friend of the consulting
party. Also a fair person's thoughts.

Ten of Hearts – Is prophetic of happiness and many children; is corrective of the bad tidings of the cards next to it, and confirms those of good ones.
Nine of Hearts – Wealth and high esteem. Also the wish card.
Eight of Hearts – Pleasure, company.
Seven of Hearts – A fickle and false friend, against whom be on your guard.
Six of Hearts – A generous but credulous person.
Five of Hearts – Troubles caused by unfounded jealousy.
Four of Hearts – A person not easily won.
Three of Hearts – Sorrow caused by a person's own imprudence.
Two of Hearts – Great success, but equal care and attention needed to secure it.
Ace of Spades – Great misfortune, spite.
King of Spades – A dark, ambitious man.
Queen of Spades – A malicious, dark women, generally a widow.
Knave of spades – An indolent, envious person; a dark man's thoughts.
Ten of Spades – Grief, imprisonment.
Nine of Spades – A card of very bad import, foretelling sickness and misfortune.
Eight of Spades – Warns a person to be cautious in his undertakings.
Seven of Spades – Loss of a friend, attended with much trouble.
Six of Spades – Wealth through industry.
Five of Spades – Shews that a bad temper requires correcting.

Four of Spades – Sickness.
Three of Spades – A journey.
Two of Spades – A removal.

Having given the signification of the various cards,
we will now proceed to describe the manner of their
employment. After having well shuffled, cut them three
times, and lay them out in rows of nine cards each. Select
any King or Queen you please to represent yourself, and
wherever you find that card placed, count nine cards every
way, reckoning it as one; and every ninth card will prove
the prophetic one. Before beginning to count, study well the
disposition of the cards, according to their individual and
relative signification. If a married woman consults the
cards, she must make her husband the King of the same
suit of which she is Queen; but if a single woman, she may
make any favourite male friend King of whatever suit she
pleases. As the Knaves of the various suits represent the
thoughts of the person represented by the picture cards of
a corresponding colour, they should also be counted from.

How to make candied angelica

Known as the 'herb of the angels', angelica is a plant
native to northern Europe, where it has been used for
many years as a tasty cake decoration or a herb in jams,
pies and crumbles. Although it has since fallen out of
fashion, Cyril Grange in his 1949 *The Complete Book of
Home Food Preservation* gives the following advice on
making one's own candied angelica.

This, as you know, is valuable for decorating and embellishing trifles, cakes, ice-creams, etc. Angelica is easy to grow (4 feet to 5 feet high), the candying is simple, and the product of first quality.

Pick stalks when green, young and tender in April.

Cut off root-ends and leaves, place stalk in basin and pour over a boiling brine (¼ oz. salt to 2 quarts water).

Allow to cook for 10 minutes, rinse in cold water, place in a saucepan of fresh boiling water and boil for 5 minutes. Drain and scrape off the outer skin.

Now comes the candying. Dissolve 1 lb. sugar in 1 pint of water, bring to boil and pour over the peel in the basin.

Candy (for 5 days soak in fresh syrup for 24 hours, then on the 6th day leave in syrup for 3 days).

Remove stalks, place on wire tray and dry in cool oven between 100° and 120°F.

Pack into bottles and store in a dry, cool, dark place.

How to hold a cocktail party

Everyone loves a party, yet the vagaries of party planning can cause many a host to come a cropper. Thankfully, *Cassell's Home Encyclopedia* (1934) has the following timeless advice on holding a cocktail party.

A cocktail party may be an informal gathering before dinner, usually from 6p.m. to 7 or 7.30p.m. or sometimes such a party is given later in the evening, when varieties of refreshments accompany the cocktail tray. These may take the form of hot toast and sandwiches, containing a mixture of grilled kipper and bloater (freed from bones and skin and sharpened with a squeeze of lemon juice and a little cayenne), or a slice of grilled bacon. Tiny squares of hot buttered toast may have a spoonful of caviar or a curled anchovy placed on them; dishes of crisp potatoes are also liked, and may be eaten with the fingers at a cocktail party. Other refreshments suitable to be served on any such occasion are finger strip sandwiches with appetising fillings such as smoked salmon or bloater cream, stuffed olives, plain biscuits buttered and spread with Gentleman's Relish, salted almonds and cheese straws.

Let us brush past the rather alarming reference to 'bloater cream' and move on to the drinks.

Many cocktails can be easily made at home. A shaker, a pair of nickel receptacles, is required to mix the ingredients properly and ensure the cocktail being cold. Crushed ice is required for most cocktails. For an almost complete outfit the mixer needs a bottle each of dry gin, whisky, brandy, pale sherry, French and Italian vermouth, Angostura bitters, orange bitters, plain sugar syrup, orange syrup, grenadine or raspberry syrup and such ingredients as oranges, lemons, eggs, tinned pineapples and soda water. When serving a dry cocktail put an olive in the glass, with a sweeter one a cherry.

Now fully *au fait* with the notion of hosting a cocktail party, perhaps readers would be advised to consult the advice on etiquette found on page 19–20 to ensure that their party flows smoothly.

How to quiet bees

One of the first skills a beekeeper must possess is knowing how to quieten a hive of bees, and *Modern Bee-Keeping: A Handbook for Cottagers* (1890) gives the following methods.

Before we can have any real pleasure amongst our bees we must learn to control them. Some are so good-tempered, that with gentle yet confident handling, we can do almost anything with them without running much risk of being stung, (this is particularly the case with pure Italian or Ligurian bees): while others are naturally irritable; but none are so cross that they cannot be subdued in the way now to be explained. All country people know how little disposed bees are to sting at swarming-time. This is because they are full of honey; and it is now well known that whenever a bee is in this condition, it will not sting unless it is actually injured.

If, then, we can make the bees fill themselves, we shall have them in our power. Blowing a little smoke amongst them will do this. It is not desirable to use tobacco, and a very little smoke will suffice. We take a roll of brown paper, or old cotton rag, or corduroy, set it smouldering, and blow some of the smoke at the hive entrance. Startled by the smoke, the bees run to their honey, and if we lift the quilt or turn up the skep [a traditional domed, woven beehive] *a minute or so afterwards, we shall find numbers of them with their heads buried in the cells, drinking it up as fast as they are able.*

Smoke, therefore, may be justly termed a bee-quieter. It is not, however, the only one. Carbolic acid has been

much used of late for the purpose of quieting bees, and
has some advantages over smoke, since it is more easy of
application, is equally effective, causes less disturbance,
and at the same time is a powerful disinfectant, and
preventative of foul brood and other disease. Much care
is required in the use of it since it is a most powerful acid,
blisters the skin, and is highly poisonous. As a bee-quieter
it is used in solution only in the following proportions:
– To a quart of warm water add one ounce of calvert's
No. 5 carbolic acid, mix well, and shake the bottle before
using. The addition of one ounce of glycerine to the
above quantities will render the solution more perfect. Its
application is very simple. A goose-quill, or small brush,
moistened with the solution, is passed over the frames as
far as the centre of the hive, when the quilt is allowed
to fall into its place. The other side of the hive is treated
similarly, and the manipulation may then commence
on either side, the brush being kept in readiness for use
when required, a few passes over the tops of the frames,

occasionally, being all that is required to keep the bees quiet.
Bees thus treated are less inclined to form clusters and to roll
off the combs than when under the influence of smoke.

A beekeeper must also have the right protective clothing,
should the bee-quieting fail:

A veil giving full protection to the face may be made of
coarse, black net. A piece of this, about 27 in. by 24 in., is
made into a bottomless bag; a hem is added round the top
and an elastic put in. This is worn over the hat, tucked in
about the neck and the coat buttoned up. The hands may be
protected by very thick woollen gloves; but they are clumsy
things, and the bees will sting them repeatedly when the
bare hands would not be attacked. All who desire to become
bee-masters will abandon gloves when they consider that
every bee that stings the gloves or hands dies, and they will
find the occasional stings they are sure to get trouble them
less and less, until, in time, neither swelling nor irritation
will follow.

If the preceding advice fails, see page 129 for how to treat
a bee sting.

How to keep ants at bay

Edmund C. P. Hull in his *The European in India* (1874)
describes quite how pervasive and intrusive the pesky ant
could become in India.

*Ants are extraordinarily numerous in India, and abound
in every place, from the high road to the bedroom. They
are principally annoying, however, in the storeroom
and pantry, of all the contents of which they will insist
on having a share, if particular pains are not taken to
exclude them. Every jam pot will be made either a barrack
for living, or a cemetery for dead ants; the bread on
being broken at table, will unexpectedly liberate a small
community; the spoons which stir one's tea, will send to the
surface some dozen victims to an over-fondness for sweets;
and so on with everything. As to sweet preserves, it will be
sometimes difficult to decide, whether fruit or ants enter
the more largely into their composition; while the cold leg
of mutton put on the breakfast table, will often require to
be brushed free of these devouring legions, If a crumb of
bread, or in fact any kind of edible, falls on the floor, it is
soon black with ant life, the smaller objects being steadily
carried off to colonies underground.*

Hull goes on to describe some rather clever methods to
keep the blighters at bay.

*The best way of keeping ants off is isolation by water;
though it is supposed they will either jump, swim, or form
a bridge across a (for them) fairly-sized canal. The legs
of the sideboard, safe, or whatever the stores are kept in,
should be set in vessels containing water; tin vessels being
sold for the purpose in the bazaars. The same plan should
be followed with beds. Pieces of rag soaked with margosa
oil,* and tied round the legs of furniture, are also said by
the natives to form an effectual bar to formic invasions.*

*Margosa oil is derived from the seeds of the Azadirachta indica tree, which is more commonly known as the neem tree in its native India and Sri Lanka. The oil has been traditionally used as an insecticide and as a remedy for asthma and arthritis. Margosa oil has an acrid smell and bitter taste and can be dangerous if ingested by young children.

How to shoe a horse

The Art of Horse-Shoeing by William Hunting (1895) is full of practical advice on how to shoe a horse. The first step is to carefully prepare the horse's foot for the fitting of the shoe.

Farriery is the art of shoeing horses, and can only be properly learned by a long practical experience in the shoeing-forge. If the foot of the horse were not a living object perhaps the training obtained in the forge would be all that was necessary for efficient workmanship. As, however, the hoof is constantly growing it is constantly changing its form. The duty of the farrier therefore is not merely to fix a shoe upon the hoof but to reduce the hoof to proper proportions before doing so.

The cheap wisdom of the amateur is often expressed in the remark 'the shoe should be fitted to the foot, not the foot to the shoe.' Like many other dogmatic statements this is only the unqualified assertion of half a truth. Foot and shoe have to be fitted to each other. There are very few horses whose feet do not require considerable alteration before a shoe can be properly fitted to them. As a rule, when a horse arrives at the forge, the feet are overgrown and quite out of proportion. In a few cases – as when a shoe has been lost on a journey – the foot is worn or broken and irregularly deficient in horn. In either instance the farrier has to make alterations in the hoof to obtain the best bearing surface before he fits a new shoe.

Once the foot has been prepared the farrier may begin to prepare the shoe.

As a material for shoes good malleable iron has no equal. It can be obtained in bars of various sizes to suit any form and weight of shoe, and the old shoes made from it may be worked up over and over again.

The chief objects to be attained in any particular pattern or form of shoe are – that it be light, easily and safely retained by a few nails, capable of wearing for three weeks or a month, and that it afford good foot-hold to the horse. All shoes should be soundly worked and free from flaws.

A shoe is first compared with the foot, it is then heated, and the heels cut off or turned down to the proper length. Each limb of the shoe is fitted to follow the outline of the wall, and it is necessary to warn the novice that the inside and outside borders of the foot are not alike.

A well fitted shoe must be fitted full to the foot … On a well-shaped foot the shoe should follow the outer line of the hoof from toe to heel, but where the heels of a foot are turned inwards there is an advantage in fitting the shoe wider at the heels, as by doing so the base of the foot is not constricted and a wider resting surface is afforded to the limb.

Provided the nail holes are properly placed, when the outside border of the shoe is fitted nicely to the circumference of the hoof, they are brought to their right position.

How to select a manure

The keen gardener or allotment keeper is well aware of the importance of fertilising the ground, and in *Practical Husbandry; or, the Art of Farming* by Dr John Trusler (1780) the many manure options are discussed.

Manuring of land is of such importance to a farmer, that he who omits it must never expect a good crop; indeed, it is the very life of husbandry, and the cultivation of land cannot go on without it.

The following is a list of manures, with the uses they are fit for, most of which are easily procured in different places.

Horse Dung: *When fresh, for cold stiff clays; when rotten, for all sorts of lands.*

Cow Dung: *Rich and cooling; fit for dry sandy ground.*

Hog Dung: *Ditto. This is rather too strong of itself, but it is an excellent mixture for the compost dunghill.*

Dung of Sheep, Rabbits, Goats, Deers &c. *Very warm, good top dressing. Folding a flock of sheep every night upon fallow ground, is a good practice. Sixty sheep will fold an acre in six weeks, equal to ten loads of dung.*

Pigeons Dung: *The hottest of most dungs, good for the compost dunghill.*

Chicken Dung: *For top dressing.*

Goose and Ducks Dung: *Ditto. Some think it spoils the grass, because horses do not like to eat where geese have fed; but this is owing to the strong salts in it.*

Human Dung: *Is of so hot a nature that it is fit only for the compost dunghill. If roch-lime be thrown into the necessary in January, it will remove the offensive smell, and dry it so to make it spread.*

Human Urine and Urine of cattle, Dogs &c. *The same quality as their respective dungs; and have this advantage, that they do not produce weeds; if mixed with as much, or two thirds water, it is a top dressing, to be sprinkled over land with water-carts.*

Dead animals: *Should be buried in compost dunghills.*

Blood from the butchers. *A very strong manure; it should be mixed with earth, sand, or saw-dust, for the convenience of carriage, and then used as a top dressing for any land.*

How to make whole-milk cheese

The lost art of making homemade cheese is here described, taken from *British Husbandry* by John Burke (1834).

The mode of making sweet-milk cheese – that is cheese made of milk which has not been skimmed – is, to put the ladder across the cheese-tub, with a large canvas cloth covering the whole, in order to prevent the falling of the milk upon the floor, or any other matter into the tub; and above this is placed the sieve through which the milk is to be strained. It should be of the temperature of 90° to 95°, and if below 85° degrees, a portion of it should be

placed in a deep brass pan, which is then immersed in the
water which is kept hot in the wash-house. By this means
the whole is warmed equally, and it is of the utmost
importance that attention be paid to it, for if the milk be
not warm enough when the rennet is put to it, the curd
will be tender, and the cheese will bulge out at the sides
... The rennet is then at once added to the milk, which is
thus coagulated at its natural heat ... The curd is then
broken into small pieces, and the whey being thoroughly
squeezed out, it is salted, wrapped in a cloth, and placed in
a chessart [the cheese-vat or container], *of such size as may*
be convenient, or is usually made in the neighbourhood; it is
then pressed with weights proportionate to its size, and turned
occasionally until it becomes sufficiently firm to be taken out
of the mould, and placed either on a cheese-rack, or on the
floor of the cheese-room, where it is occasionally turned,
and dry rubbed with salt, and remains until fit for market.

How to preserve eggs

Many families keep their own chickens in order to have
fresh eggs aplenty; however there are times of year (such
as when the birds are moulting) when the birds may not
lay – so to ensure a steady supply of eggs the householder
would be advised to preserve some in times of glut. Cyril
Grange, in his 1949 *The Complete Book of Home Food
Preservation*, details the following method.

It is important that every egg to be preserved is of suitable
quality. It must be new-laid (under 7 days old), clean

*(preferably unwashed), firm, even, strong and smooth of shell,
and preferably infertile (that is, laid by unmated hens).*

*Water Glass: The selected eggs are packed large end
up in the vessel and the prepared solution either poured
on or the eggs lowered in the basket into the solution. The
solution is made by dissolving 1 lb. of water glass* [sodium
silicate] *in 1 gallon of boiled and cooled soft water, and
this is correct for 100 eggs.*

*The solution must cover the topmost layer of eggs to
a depth of at least 2 inches to allow for evaporation. It is
better to put the eggs in the preserve as they are collected
daily than to wait until sufficient have been collected to fill
the vessel.*

*Having packed and filled, the vessel must be covered
with a double thickness cover of close-woven material to
exclude dust and retard evaporation. The vessel is then
taken to a cool, airy, dry place. To use, merely wash with
water first.*

How to create an artificial swarm of bees

When beekeepers wish to move a bee colony to a new
hive, or split an existing colony, they must cause the
bees to swarm (whereby the queen bee and a number of
worker bees leave the hive together to form a new colony).
Practical Bee-Keeping by Frank Cheshire (1878) advises
the following methods for creating an artificial swarm.

*The bees' natural means of increase, 'swarming', demands
so much time, and is accompanied by so much uncertainty*

*and inconvenience, that but few apiculturists nowadays
have not taken the matter altogether into their own hands,
increasing the number of their colonies by a variety of
methods called generally 'artificial swarming.'*

*It is needless to point out that, left to themselves, swarms
now and again settle in most inconvenient positions, or
come off at most inconvenient times, or are lost by leaving
when no watcher is at hand.*

*Before we can swarm artificially with hives with fixed
combs, it is necessary for us to understand the art of
drumming or driving bees from their house and home, so
as to place them at our disposal. The plan usually followed
may be thus described: The skep [a traditional domed,
woven beehive] to be drummed has a puff or two of smoke
from tobacco, burning rag, or smouldering wood driven
into its mouth, so as to frighten its inhabitants, and cause
them to fill themselves with honey. The hive is lifted from
its floorboard and turned bottom upwards upon a tub or
pail, so that it has a firm standing; upon it is placed an
empty skep having exactly the same diameter as itself;
a jack towel or bandage of some description is fastened
around the edges of the two hives in such a way that not
a bee can escape. The lower hive i.e., the one containing
combs and bees, is now beaten with sticks or by the hands,
so as to jar the whole fabric and terrify the bees, whose
composure has already been upset by the smoke blown
amongst them. The beating must be continuous, but not
violent, or we are likely to break the combs from their
attachments, and so merely bury our bees in the ruins of
their city. In from one to five minutes they will be found
rushing, whilst making a roaring noise by vibrating their*

wings, into the upper hive, from the roof of which, upon separating the two, they will be found hanging much like a natural swarm.

Having given a puff of smoke, remove it from its stand, upon which place an empty decoy skep to receive and amuse the bees returning from the fields. Drum the stock, and watch careful for the ascent of the queen. A quick eye will rarely allow her to pass unnoticed, but if she has not been seen, turn over the hive containing the swarm (technically the forced swarm), for an examination, and if her majesty does not shew herself shake the bees sharply round, when they will roll over each other like so many grocer's currants, and the object of our search will be thrown to the top and detected amongst them. As they crawl (for they will into fly) up the side of the hive, and cluster thickly upon it, beat them down by a sharp rap on the outside of it. Repeating the operation a few times, we can hardly fail in discovering, if present, the mother, in spite of her attempts at concealment behind her retreating children. The queen being found, place the forced swarm upon the old stand, and shake out the bees that have in the meantime returned to the decoy hive from the fields, when they will enter their new abode, and, finding their queen, will, with the rest, commence comb building at once, as would a natural swarm.

How to run a household in Anglo-India

For the British expatriate arriving in India for the first time, it must have been quite a culture shock. Many books were written to lend genteel Brits tips and hints on how to make the smooth transition into Anglo-Indian life. One such book, *The European in India* by Edmund C. P. Hull (1874), went so far as to list the number of servants ordinarily required to run a household in Anglo-India.

The following is intended to be a list of servants required in the house of a married couple, without children, in comfortable pecuniary circumstances: —
1, Butler; 2, matey; 3, boy, or dressing-boy; 4, ayah; 5, cook; 6, cook's matey, or market-boy; 7, tannycatch;* 8, waterman; 9, totee, or sweeper; 10, and 11, two gardeners; 12, a bearer (two are sometimes employed); 13, punkahman,** for day work; 14, and 15, two punkahman, for night work (for each bedroom); and supposing the stable establishment to consist of a one-horse office carriage, and an open carriage and pair for evening drives, the following additional servants — 16, coachman (perhaps two); 17, 18 and 19, three horsekeepers; 20, 21 and 22, three grasscutters (women).
The above list gives a complement of 18 men and 5 women servants; costing from 135 to 150 rupees a month.

* A Tannycatch was the equivalent of a scullery maid, assisting the cook in tasks such as boiling water and grinding rice.
** A punkah is a type of large ceiling fan; the punkahwallah is the person who operates said fan by pulling on a system of pulleys.

Hull went on to reveal his disdain for the sheer numbers of servants employed in the Anglo-Indian household.

A Calcutta resident wrote to me lately as follows: — 'The number of our servants is simply ridiculous, and the work

each has to do hardly appreciable. It would be a great blessing if the number of idle hangers-on in every house, could be diminished.' An opinion in which, I imagine, all will coincide.

How to perform tricks with coins

Modern Magic: A Practical Treatise on the Art of Conjuring by Professor Hoffmann (*c.* 1904) contains the following pleasingly simple coin tricks with which to amaze and delight your friends and relations.

A Florin being spun upon the table, to tell blindfold whether it falls head or tail upwards − *You borrow a florin and spin it, or invite some other person to spin it, on the table (which must be without a cloth). You allow it to spin itself out, and immediately announce, without seeing it, whether it has fallen head or tail upwards. This may be repeated a number of times with the same result, though you may be blindfolded, and placed at the further end of the apartment.*

The secret lies in the use of a florin of your own, on one face of which (say on the 'tail' side) you have cut at the extreme edge a little notch, thereby causing a minute point or tooth of metal to project from that side of the coin. If a coin so prepared be spun on the table, and should chance go down with the notched side upwards, it will run down like an ordinary coin, with a long continuous 'whirr,' the sound growing fainter and fainter till it finally ceases; But if it should run down with the notched side downwards,

*the friction of the point against the table will reduce this
final whirr to half its ordinary length, and the coin will go
down with a sort of 'flop.' The difference of sound is not
sufficiently marked to attract the notice of the spectators,
but is perfectly distinguishable by an attentive ear.*

Odd or even, or the mysterious addition – *This is a
trick of almost childish simplicity, depending upon an
elementary arithmetical principle. We have, however,
known it to occasion great perplexity, even to more than
ordinarily acute persons.*

*You take a handful of coins or counters, and invite
another person to do the same, and to ascertain privately
whether the number he has taken is odd or even. You request
the company to observe that you have not asked him a single
question, but that you are able, notwithstanding, to divine
and counteract his most secret intentions, and that you
will in proof of this, yourself take a number of coins,
and add them to those he has taken, when, if his number
was odd, the total shall be even; if his number was even,
the total shall be odd. Requesting him to drop the coins
he holds into a hat, held on high by one of the company,
your drop in a certain number on your own account. He is
now asked whether his total was odd or even; and, the coins
being counted, the total number proves to be, as you stated,
exactly the reverse. The experiment is tried again and
again, with different numbers, but the result is the same.*

*The secret lies in the simple arithmetical fact, that if
you add an odd number to an even number the result will
be odd; if you add an odd number to an odd number the
result will be even. You have only to take care, therefore,*

that the number you yourself add, whether large or small,
shall always be odd.

To make a marked sixpence vanish from a handkerchief,
and be found in the centre of an apple or orange,
previously examined – *Have ready, concealed in either*
hand, a sixpence of your own, with a little wax smeared
on one side of it. Roll another minute portion of wax into
a round ball half the size of a peppercorn, and press it
lightly upon the lowest button of your waistcoat, so that
you may be able to find it instantly when wanted. You
must, also have at hand an ordinary full-sized table-knife
and a plate of oranges.
  You begin by borrowing a sixpence (requesting the
owner to mark it) and a handkerchief. You spread the
handkerchief flat on the table, with its sides square with
those of the table. Then standing behind your table,
you place ostensibly the borrowed sixpence, but really
your own (with the waxed side up), in the centre of the
handkerchief, then fold over the corners, one by one,
beginning with one of those nearest to yourself, in such
manner that each shall overlap the sixpence by about
an inch, gently pressing each corner as you fold it down.
Ask some one to come forward, and ascertain by feeling
the handkerchief, that the sixpence is really there. Then
offer the knife for inspection, and after all are satisfied
that it is without preparation, hand the plate of oranges
to be examined in like manner, requesting the audience
to choose one for the purpose of the trick. While they do
so, your fingers go in search of the little ball of wax, and
press it against one side of the marked sixpence, which still

remains in your hand. Press the sixpence against one side of the blade of the knife, at about the middle of its length, and lay the knife on the table, the sixpence adhering to its under side. Then taking hold of the handkerchief and blowing on its centre, draw the hands quickly apart. The two corners of the side next to you will thus be brought one into each hand, and adhering to one of them (the one which you first folded down), will be the substitute sixpence, which will thus appear to have vanished. Hand the handkerchief for examination that it may be seen that the coin has really disappeared, and meanwhile get rid of the substitute into your pocket or elsewhere. Turn up your sleeves, and show that your hands are empty. Then take up the knife (taking care to keep the side on which the sixpence is away from the spectators), and cut open the orange. Cut about half way with the point, and then finish the cut by drawing the whole length of the blade through the opening thus made. This will detach the sixpence, which will fall between the two halves of the orange, as though it had all along been contained therein. Wipe it with the handkerchief to remove the juice of the orange from it, and at the same time rub off any wax which may still adhere to it, and hand it for identification.

How to make a paste for chapped hands

A Shilling's Worth of Practical Receipts (1856) includes the following instructions for making a paste to soothe sore, chapped hands.

Mix a quarter of a pound of unsalted hog's lard, which has been washed in water, and then in rose water, with the yolks of two new laid eggs, add a large spoonful of honey. Add as much fine oatmeal, or almond paste, as will work it into a paste.

How to make conversation

The lost art of conversation is never more mourned than at a grindingly boring gathering where people are attempting to make small talk. *All About Etiquette: or The Manners of Polite Society for Ladies, Gentlemen, and Families* (1879) contains a great deal of excellent advice on how to charm in conversation.

One is quite sure to show good or bad breeding the instant the mouth is opened to talk in company. If he is a gentleman he starts no subject of conversation that can possibly be displeasing to any person present. The ground is common to all, and no one has a right to monopolize any part of it for his own particular opinions, in politics or religion. No one is there to make proselytes, but everyone has been invited to be agreeable and to please.

At such times you should avoid appearing dogmatical and too positive in any assertions you make which can possibly be subject to any contradiction. He who is peremptory in his own story may meet with another as positive as himself to contradict him, and then the two positives will be sure to have a skirmish.

You will forbear to interrupt a person who is telling a story, even if he is making historical mistakes in date and facts. If he makes mistakes it is his own fault, and it is not your business to mortify him by attempting to correct his blunders in presence of those with whom he is ambitious to stand well.

A sure way to please in conversation is to hunt up as many of each other's excellences as possible, and be as blind as possible to each other's imperfections. There is no compromise of this principle in this, for you are to consider that a social party is not intended as a school for reform, or a pulpit to denounce sin.

Avoid railing and sarcasm in social parties; they are weapons which few can use. Malicious jests, at the expense of those who are present or absent, show that he who used them is devoid both of the instincts and habits of a gentleman.

Even if you are not a good talker try to sustain some share of the conversation; for you as easily insult a company by maintaining a contemptuous silence as by engrossing all the talk. Listen attentively and patiently to what is said. It is a great and difficult talent to be a good listener, but it is one which the well-bred man has to acquire at whatever pains.

How to wash

With the advent of the power shower many have lost the skill of the toilette. Fortunately, *The Handbook of the Toilette* (1839) provides some excellent instruction.

On rising in the morning, if the sponge be used for
ablution, the body should be divested of the garments
worn during the night, and skin fully exposed to the
atmosphere of the dressing-room. The body should then
be sponged over the whole of its surface, and immediately
rubbed dry with rough towels. Let not the delicate lady
forego this – her skin will be improved by the friction …
If cold water be used, and it produce a feeling of heat
– or, more correctly speaking, a glow all over the body
– affording a sensation of pleasurable warmth, the cold
water should have the preference: but if, after its use, there
is a feeling of chilliness and languor, the skin has not the
power to react, and the water should be lukewarm. After
the body has been rubbed dry, friction should be applied
with a flesh-brush, and the whole person enveloped, so long
as convenience requires it, in a flannel wrapper.

The surface of the body being thus washed and rubbed,
there remain other parts to undergo a more formal sort
of washing, in which soap is a necessary agent. Of these,
the feet should be washed first. The water should be tepid,
though some prefer it cold. This, in winter, is decidedly
bad; and, in that season, immersion for a few minutes in
water almost as cold as the air, may cause considerable
injury. Each part of the body, as it is washed, should be
dried with a coarse, in preference to a fine towel.

In a book which I lately read, a learned physician
is quoted as having recommended that the head should
never be washed, and the feet as seldom as possible. Such
advice is outrageously absurd, – and the doctor for whom
it emanated, must needs be, or have been, a very disgusting
person. The feet should be washed EVERY DAY, – so

should *EVERY OTHER PART* of the body, except
the head.

Once a week, a warm bath should be taken, about five or
six degrees hotter than the body, the temperature of which
may be ascertained by holding, for a few minutes, the bulb
of a small thermometer under the tongue. After remaining
a quarter of an hour in the bath, the whole surface of the
body should be well rubbed with fine soap and a flannel, or
with almond paste, which is again to be washed off. After
the soaping, it is advisable to remain in the bath another
half hour. Persons who can afford more than ordinary
luxuries, may have a second bath close at hand, into which
a bottle of Eau de Cologne, or any other perfume, has been
poured; and, after the soaping is over, and the soap washed
off, they may step from the first bath into the second, where
they should remain half an hour.

To make the skin supple and soft, or to restore it to
proper condition, if rough, – to free it, in short, from those
impurities which are often the consequence of neglecting
this organ, and charge loveliness of feature and beauty of
form, with unseemly cutaneous eruptions, it may be rubbed
with the following preparation instead of soap. Boil in soft
water a dozen pounds of barley-meal and four pounds of
bran, until the whole is of the consistence of thick cream.
When this is washed off, almond paste may be used, and
the second bath resorted to immediately. For ordinary
periodical bathing, however, one bath and a good soaping,
are quite sufficient.

How to borrow things politely

Most people will admit that they have an item that they have borrowed from friends or neighbours stashed in their garage, awaiting return. This timeless problem has happily been addressed by *All About Etiquette: or The Manners of Polite Society for Ladies, Gentlemen, and Families* (1879) which advises the following rules of borrowing.

Buy any article you are likely to want on more than one occasion rather than borrow. If your own, you can always have it at hand; you will lay yourself under no obligation to a lender and incur no responsibility as to its safety while in your possession. But when you do borrow, see that the article is speedily returned. And under no consideration take the liberty of lending it to any person whatever before restoring it to the owner. Apologies and expressions of regret are no compensation, should it be out of your power to replace it if injured or lost.

No articles are more frequently borrowed than umbrellas, and none are returned with so little punctuality. Frequently a borrowed umbrella is never thought of by the borrower till after the weather clears up, the lender most probably suffering inconvenience for want of it. Often, it is detained till the next rain, when the lender has to take the trouble of sending for it. And then it is very possible it may not be found at all, some person in the meantime having nefariously carried it off. In such a case it is a matter of common honesty for the careless borrower to replace that umbrella with a new one, as she is not to suppose that empty expression of regret or unmeaning apologies will be sufficient compensation for a substantial loss.

If, in consequence of the unexpected arrival of company, anything for the table as borrowed, such as tea, coffee &c., see that it is punctually returned, equal in quantity and in quality, or rather superior. Habitual borrowers are very apt to forget this piece of honesty, either neglecting to return the things at all or meanly substituting inferior articles.

How to read the future from tea or coffee grounds

After a nice cup of tea or coffee it is always pleasant to have a quick peek into the future, and *A Handbook of Cartomancy: Fortune-telling and Occult Divination* by Grand Orient (1889) explains the method.

Pour the grounds of tea or coffee into a white cup; shake them well about, so as to spread them over the surface; reverse the cup to drain away the superfluous contents, and then exercise your intuitive and previsional powers in discovering what the resultant figures represent. Long, wavy lines denote vexations and losses, their importance depending on the number of lines. Straight ones on the contrary, foretell peace, tranquillity, and long life. Human figures are usually good omens, announcing love affairs and marriages. If circular figures predominate, the person for whom the experiment is made may expect to receive money. If these circles are connected by straight, unbroken lines, there will be delay, but ultimately all will be satisfactory. Squares foretell peace and happiness; oblong figures, family discord; curved, twisted, or angular ones, are certain signs of vexations and annoyances – their probable duration being determined by the number of figures. A number of lines, whether long or short, foretell a happy old age. A crown signifies honour, and for politicians &c., success at court. A cross denotes news of death, but three in the same cup are symbolical of honour. A ring means marriage; if a letter can be discovered near it, that will be the initial of the name of the future spouse. If the ring be in the clear part of the cup, it foretells a happy union; if there are clouds about it, expect the contrary; if it chance to be quite at the bottom the marriage will never take place … Quadrupeds – with the exception of the dog – foretell trouble and difficulties; reptiles mean treachery. Fish imply good news from across the water, but some authorities interpret their appearance as the presage of an invitation to a good dinner.